ROAD TRIP SEATTLE TO YELLOWSTONE

BY DOUGLAS SCOTT

TABLE OF CONTENTS

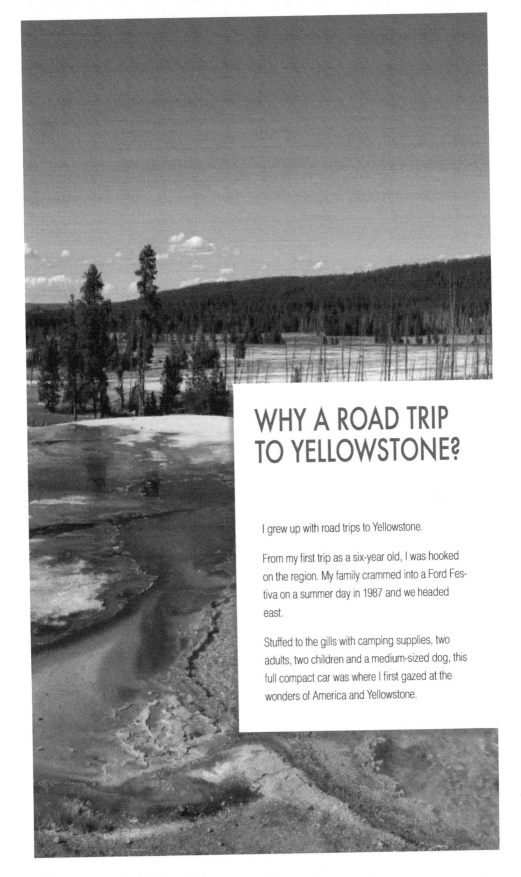

WHY A ROAD TRIP TO YELLOWSTONE?

I grew up with road trips to Yellowstone.

From my first trip as a six-year old, I was hooked on the region. My family crammed into a Ford Festiva on a summer day in 1987 and we headed east.

Stuffed to the gills with camping supplies, two adults, two children and a medium-sized dog, this full compact car was where I first gazed at the wonders of America and Yellowstone.

Our family trips to Yellowstone became yearly, and they opened my eyes to the beauty of the Northwest and Yellowstone National Park.

Road trips are a part of American's identity. Being able to drive from Washington State to Montana and Wyoming, across the mighty Rocky Mountains and over the Continental Divide is an incredible experience that everyone should have, at least once. The drive to Yellowstone takes you from the edge of a temperate rainforest, through the desolation of Eastern Washington, through the pine forests of Northern Idaho and into the land we all know as Big Sky Country.

The drive to Yellowstone from Seattle is a drive for fans of nature, history, Americana, and the spirit of the West. With each unique region along the drive, the path to Yellowstone retraces many of the steps Lewis and Clark took in 1804 while exploring.

DISTANCE

Depending on your route, the distance to Yellowstone from Seattle varies. We suggest taking Interstate 90 and then either going to West Yellowstone or Gardiner, Montana.

If you leave from Seattle and drive to West Yellowstone with no detours, it is 739 miles and will take you about 12 hours of driving time.

If you leave from Seattle and drive to Gardiner with no detours, it is 754 miles and will take you about 11 hours of driving time.

Once at Yellowstone, be prepared to easily put on 300 or 400 more miles on your car, as you will want to drive around the park, explore The Grand Tetons and take small detours along the way.

TERRAIN OF THE DRIVE

The terrain along the road to Yellowstone varies, depending on which climate region you are entering. For ease of understanding, we have broken the drive up into five easy to distinguish areas.

Western Washington

This section of the drive is mostly uphill, as you are climbing the Cascade Range and moving toward a much dryer climate.

Eastern Washington

Considered by many to be the most boring part of the drive, eastern Washington is mostly flat and mostly farmland. While many try to speed through this section, take some time and enjoy the stops we list. Eastern Washington is actually pretty cool, no matter what most Seattle-ites say.

Northern Idaho: aka North Idaho

North Idaho reminds me of the original Oregon Trail computer game hunting missions. Rocks and pine trees line the road, occasionally showing off awesome rivers and lakes, as well as showing off the rich mining history of the region. You will continuously gain elevation in Idaho, as the border to Montana is at the top of Lookout Pass.

Montana Forests

From Lookout Pass to Missoula, the drive along Interstate 90 is mostly following Clark's Fork, a winding river that carved out a lower route to the West. The drive through here is mountainous and scenic, much like the proceeding region of Northern Idaho.

Big Sky Country

From Missoula to Yellowstone, the trees become sparse and visibility increases. Rolling hills expand the landscape and antelope run next to the Interstate. While animals are numerous along the drive, the terrain of Big Sky Country amplifies the beauty of the area. This section is wide open and intoxicating, and it is easy to see why so many have called this region home.

WEATHER

Spring

Expect snow along the drive through June. Temperatures in the passes can drop well below freezing. However, Interstate 90 is well maintained and about as safe as you can get for such a huge freeway.

Summer

During the summer months, you may encounter heavy rain and occasional thunderstorms. During the day it will be hot, up to the 90 degree Fahrenheit range, but at night the temperature can drop to below freezing.

Fall

Fall is similar to spring, as snow can, and will, fall at any time. The pass is well maintained, but early snow may cause delays or temporary closures. Heavy rains may also occur. Generally, the temperature is chilly, but mild.

Winter

During the winter months, driving to Yellowstone from Seattle can be tough, especially during periods of heavy rain and snow. If you plan to drive during the winter, expect to drive extremely slowly. Buy chains for your vehicle, even if it is 4-wheel drive. Also, check conditions and be prepared to stay the night somewhere if a pass is deemed dangerous. Check DOT conditions when possible.

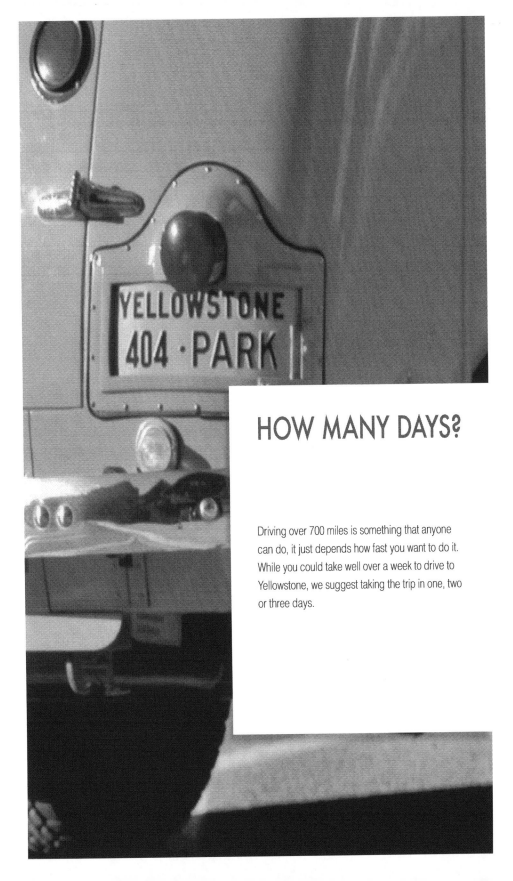

HOW MANY DAYS?

Driving over 700 miles is something that anyone can do, it just depends how fast you want to do it. While you could take well over a week to drive to Yellowstone, we suggest taking the trip in one, two or three days.

ONE DAY

Driving straight through is only for those who enjoy driving and are in a hurry to get to Yellowstone. Typically, stops are few and far between, focusing less on the fun of the road trip, but instead on the destination.

This drive is easily doable in one day, just expect to wake up early and arrive late. It usually takes about 12 hours, and if you pack your meals and stop only for gas and to use the bathroom, this drive flies by. This itinerary is only recommended for experienced solo drivers or those parties who have numerous drivers willing to drive for a few hours at a time. However, keep in mind that there is a time change!

TWO DAYS

This is the recommended allotment for driving to Yellowstone. With a two-day itinerary, one is able to get in to Missoula or Deer Lodge for a night and explore a few sights along the way. It also gives you plenty of time to get to the park early enough to see if any of the remote campgrounds have open sites.

Driving in two days is recommended for both health and sanity reasons. Sitting in a car for 11 or 12 hours at once is tough for most people. Breaking up the trip allows for stops at visitor centers, small towns, museums and roadside attractions. We HIGHLY recommend doing this.

THREE DAYS

If you really love stopping at numerous attractions and destinations, driving to Yellowstone in three days makes the most sense. By breaking it up into three days, you guarantee yourself a relaxing journey full of great side trips. Three days from Seattle to Yellowstone is a road trippers dream, since you are able to hike, explore and leisurely enjoy the sights of this amazing drive.

THE ANIMALS YOU WILL SEE

ANIMALS ALONG THE DRIVE

While Yellowstone National Park will obviously have more animals than the drive to the park it-self, the amount of wildlife along the route to America's original National Park is quite impressive. In fact, the list is so awesome that we compiled the "12 Best Animals to See Along the Road."

Watching for wildlife can be a great way to pass time on this road trip. Watching for animals during the trip is also a great way to get your eyes used to scanning the landscape for animals, a common practice while exploring Yellowstone.

ELK

COYOTE

BALD EAGLE

ANTELOPE

MOOSE

11

GRIZZLY BEAR

COUGAR

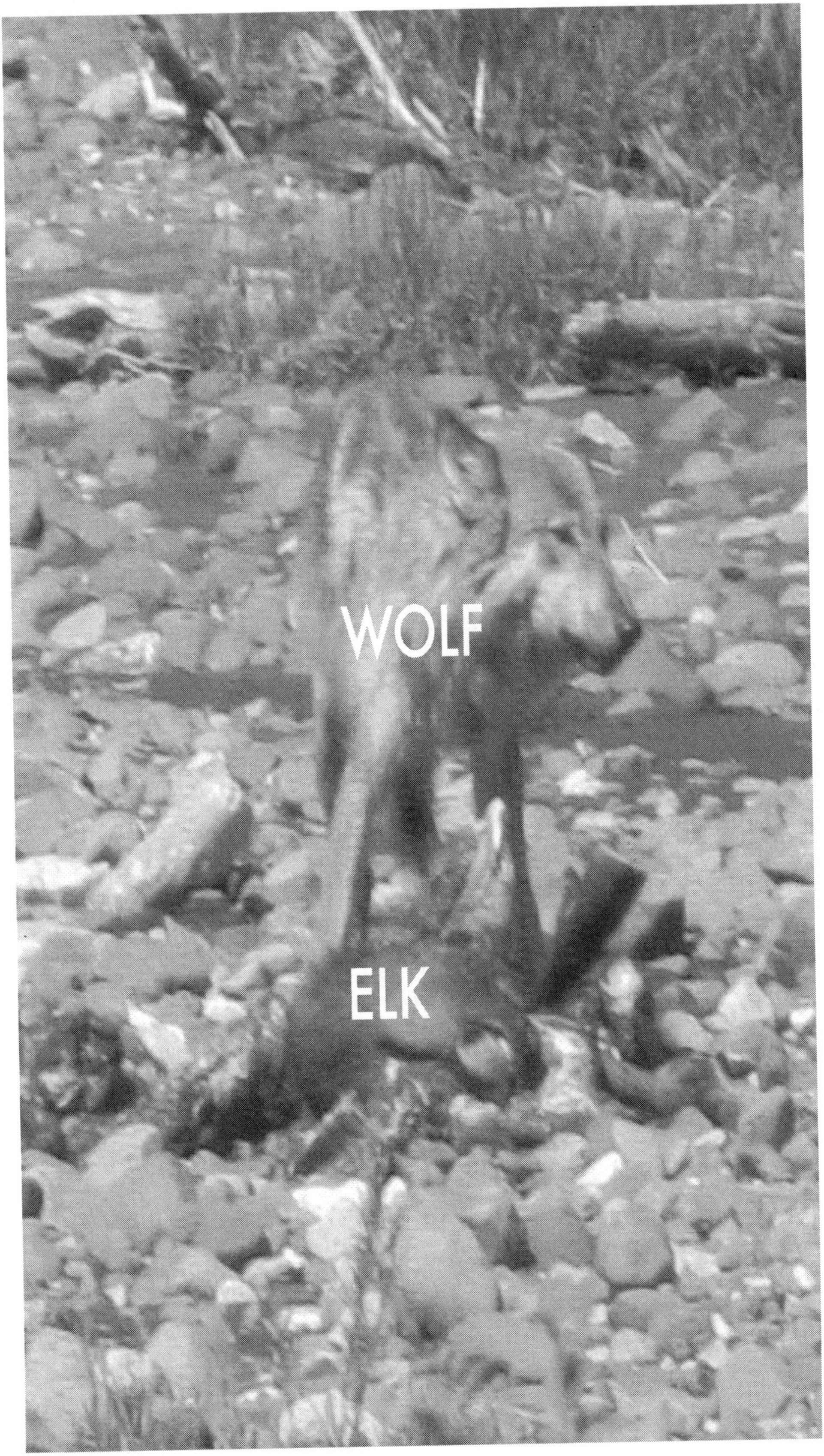
WOLF
ELK

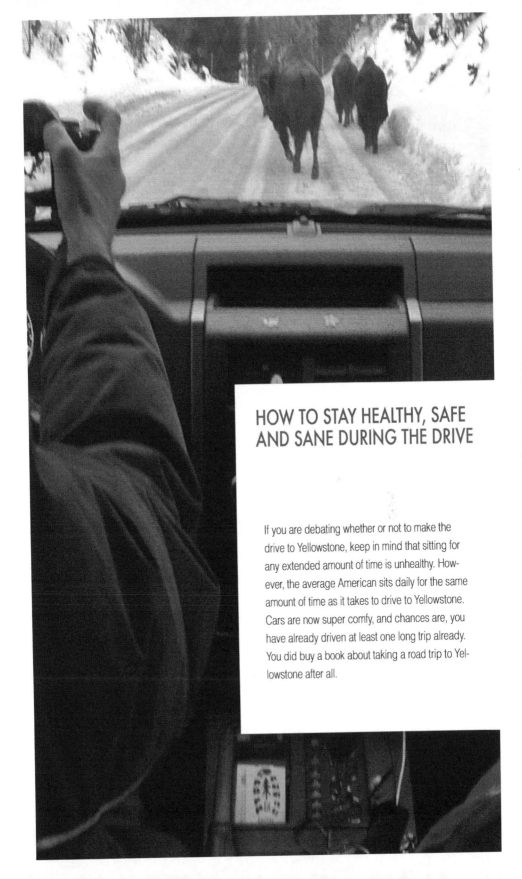

HOW TO STAY HEALTHY, SAFE AND SANE DURING THE DRIVE

If you are debating whether or not to make the drive to Yellowstone, keep in mind that sitting for any extended amount of time is unhealthy. However, the average American sits daily for the same amount of time as it takes to drive to Yellowstone. Cars are now super comfy, and chances are, you have already driven at least one long trip already. You did buy a book about taking a road trip to Yellowstone after all.

While we want you to get to Yellowstone and all the other stops along the way as quickly as possible, we also want you to be as healthy and safe as possible. We recommend taking numerous breaks, stopping to stretch, eating properly and staying well-hydrated.

Drivers

If you are going on this trip solo, be smart and be safe. Take breaks, get enough sleep, eat good food and stay hydrated. If at any time you feel drowsy, lightheaded, or if you are just feeling "off," take a break, get out of the car and get some food. If you need to stop for the day: **STOP**!

If you have more than one driver, set driving limits of mileage, destination or time. Be realistic and be safe. Everyone should drive equally, unless there is a reason not to do so. Road trips can be stressful if one person feels they have driven too much, so reduce resentment and help drive!

Also, the driver gets to decide on the music. This is a rule.

Stops

We recommend stopping once every three to four hours, minimum. Stops mean getting out of your car and walking around for at least 15 minutes. This can be at a scenic spot, a rest area, a gas station or even one of the many gas station casinos you will encounter once you enter Montana. The main purpose for stops are to get fresh air, stretch your legs, and get your blood flowing.

Foods

Stereotypically, people on road trips eat poorly, but many of us actually bring fresh fruits and vegetables with us, as well as Twinkies, whole-grain chips, nuts, cheeses and Red Bull.

To pack food for the road trip, start with thinking of comfort foods. Chips, sandwiches, apples and bananas are a great start, as are fruit snacks, beef jerky and a veggie tray. Try to stay away from foods that will give you gas. Seriously, you will be sitting in a car for hours.

When possible, try to avoid foods with high sugar contents, as that will lead to sugar crash while driving.

Games

On long car trips, we often play a game called "The Three." In this game, you hypothetically decided which three foods you could consume for the rest of your life. Basically, you have to try to figure out how to remain healthy while never being able to vary your diet.

Example: Chicken, wheat bread and vegetable soup. (It won't work because you will get scurvy)

Another great game is the "Alphabet Game." While many variations exist on this classic road trip car game, there is only one correct way to play the game. The rules are simple. Using signs (not writing on cars, trucks or license plates) you must find letters A through Z before the other players. Each letter on a sign can only be used once.

Document the Trip

By all means, document every aspect of this trip. Take videos, live tweet, write down funny sayings that come from the trip and use social media to share it all. Create a #hashtag, as we usually do, to let those not lucky enough to join you follow your progress and share in your wonder, boredom, wit and adventure.

While it might seem annoying at first, documenting the trip will be something you will be glad you did years from now. Imagine if you could relive all of your childhood road trips through your phone. Try it and your future self will be stoked you did.

License Plate Game

To pass the time on the trip, you can always play the time tested "License Plate Game." With 50 States, make a list and keep track of how many states you will see. While rules can be changed, moving trucks and semis do not count. By the time you are leaving Yellowstone, you likely should have seen all 50.

THE BEST STOPS ON THE TRIP

With nearly 800 miles of driving, it is hard to always know what the best side-trip is along the route to Yellowstone. From fruit stands and state parks to National Wildlife Refuges and caverns, one may feel overwhelmed with the choices in front of them. As experts on the road to Yellowstone, we are pleased to give you the best of the best.

Over the next chapter, you will get an insight into the best locations to drive to when heading to Yellowstone. While you could
just drive straight through to the park, exploring the culture, history, nature and quirkiness that the road to Yellowstone has to offer is almost as good as the park itself.

From Eastern Washington to the towns on the outer edges of Yellowstone National Park, the entire drive is awesome. In the following pages, we share with you eleven must-see stops and eleven
awesome roadside attractions.

Whether you choose one or choose all 22, you won't be disappointed

DIRECTIONS: EXIT 136 ON
INTERSTATE 90 IN
WASHINGTON STATE. UPON
EXITING, HEAD NORTH
VANTAGE HIGHWAY,
FOLLOWING THE SIGNS TO
GINGKO PETRIFIED FOREST
STATE PARK.

SIZE: 7,000 ACRES

FEES: STATE PARK ENTRANCE
FEES

HIGHLIGHTS: PETRIFIED
WOOD, PETROGLYPHS,
SCENIC VIEWS

FUN FACT: WASHINGTON
STATE'S OFFICIAL GEM IS
PETRIFIED WOOD

Ginkgo Petrified Forest State Park

Standing along the rugged Columbia River Gorge, Gingko Petrified Forest State Park is often passed by the millions of drivers
heading east and west. Those who drive by without stopping at
the perfectly situated park along the banks of the Columbia River
are missing out on a historical and geological wonder within two
hours of Seattle.

Washington State's Gingko Petrified Forest State Park is an awesome place to stretch your legs at the start of your road trip. With
the largest collection of petrified wood in the state, as well as
nearly 60 well-preserved petroglyphs on display in the interpre-
tive center and along the trail, stopping here is like stepping
back in time. Looking over the well-carved out canyon of the Columbia River, it is easy to see why this place has been home to
humans for thousands of years.

The park is located on the old stomping grounds of the Wanapum Tribe, now known as the Confederated Tribes and Bands of the Yakima Nation. Wanapum, in the native language of Sahaptin, translates to River People, and standing anywhere along the four miles of trails in the state park, it is easy to see why.

With two trails, one 1.5 miles and the other 2.5 miles long, taking a short trek here gets your trip off to a great start. The trail winds its way along the old banks of Lake Vantage, a prehistoric lake no longer in existence, next to 22 species of petrified wood. Walking along the bluffs, above the Columbia River, these short trails get you in the mindset to truly appreciate the geology and history of the area.

With sweeping views of the Columbia River Gorge, this is your first "dry" stop on your journey to Yellowstone. It can be raining and 45 degrees Fahrenheit in Seattle, while 90 degrees and sunny in Vantage. Stopping here is sure to lift not only your spirits as far as warmth and happiness, but it also is the best way to kick off your spirit of adventure.

DIRECTIONS:
EXIT 136 ON INTERSTATE 90
IN WASHINGTON STATE.
UPON EXITING, HEAD NORTH
ON VANTAGE HIGHWAY,
FOLLOWING THE SIGNS TO
GINGKO PETRIFIED FOREST
STATE PARK.

SIZE: 198FT

FEES: STATE PARK ENTRANCE
FEES

HIGHLIGHTS: HIKING,
PHOTOGRAPHY LOCATIONS,
PICNIC SPOTS, GIANT
AWESOME WATERFALL

FUN FACT: THIS IS
WASHINGTON STATE'S
OFFICIAL WATERFALL

Palouse Falls State Park

Before we explain this awesome location, please be aware that heading to this destination is quite a detour from the normal route to Yellowstone. The trip to Palouse Falls will add a minimum of two and half hours to your already 11 hour trip. Don't let that scare you from seeing the falls though, as Palouse Falls was just recently named the Official Waterfall of Washington State.

Originally named Aputaput, Palouse Falls is a great place to spend the day, take some pictures and eat a lunch, all while staring at the sheer power and force that water has on the land. Waterfalls are gorgeous, exciting and even educational. We feel Palouse Falls is the perfect way to showcase the greatness and variety of Washington State. While most people know Washington for Mount Rainier, the Olympic National Park and Seattle, Palouse Falls in Eastern Washington is one of the most memorable locations in the state.

With a two mile hiking trail that only gains 293 feet, this is a fantastic, family-friendly hike to a magnificent waterfall. With picnic tables, a paved trail and a secondary trail to a more fantastic viewpoint, visiting Palouse State Park needs to be added to any modern explorer's list.

If you are interested in geology, the cliffs and canyons that make Palouse Falls spectacular were carved out by a giant flood that occurred when the Missoula Ice Dam broke apart in the Pleistocene Epoch. The floods shaped the entire region, including the mighty Columbia River, and occurred between 15,000 and 13,000 years ago.

DIRECTIONS: IN IDAHO, TAKE
EXIT 15 TOWARD SHERMAN
AVE. MERGE ONTO NORTH
23RD STREET, CONTINUE
ONTO EAST COEUR D'ALENE
LAKE DRIVE

SIZE: 25 MILES LONG WITH
109 MILES OF SHORELINE

FEES: NONE

HIGHLIGHTS: PHOTOGRAPHY
LOCATIONS, PICNIC SPOTS,
LAKE VIEWS

FUN FACT: DURING THE FALL
MONTHS, THIS AREA IS ONE
OF THE BUSIEST SPOTS FOR

BALD EAGLES IN NORTH
IDAHO.

Higgens Point

Many will stop in Coeur d'Alene and explore the marina district in
downtown CDA, we recommend skipping the traffic and the
crowds and head to the most underrated parks in the area. With
eagles and salmon instead of boats and people, this park at the
end of the 23 mile Centennial Trail is a fantastic way to get a
grasp on the size and scope of North Idaho's wilderness.

Considered by many to be one of the best kept secrets in all of North Idaho, Higgens Point is easy to get to and beautiful year-round. Right off the freeway and located on a small outcropping of land along the shores of Lake Coeur d'Alene, this park is an excellent spot for a picnic lunch and a short walk. While the parking lot is close to Interstate 90, a short walk to the end of the point will leave you isolated from the motorists zooming along.

Lake Coeur d'Alene was formed during the Missoula Floods of 13,000 to 15,000 years ago. As the glaciers were retreating, a huge ice dam was formed near present-day Missoula. When the dam burst, the floods formed numerous recognizable features, including Lake Coeur d'Alene and the Columbia River Gorge.

Rumors swirl in town about the lake holding the remains of numerous Model T automobiles. Supposedly, the cars sunk in the early 1900s when locals would drive across the lake during the winter as a short-cut to driving around the lake. While not confirmed, standing at Higgens Point, it is easy to see why the locals would have taken that risk. The lake is 25 miles long and has over 109 miles of shoreline.

Directions:
Mile Marker 61 on Interstate 90

Wallace, Idaho

Size: 784 people

Fees: None

Highlights: History, Museums, Mining
Tours, 9 taverns

Fun Fact: In 2004, Wallace was designated by the mayor to be the center of the Universe, placing a plaque in town to honor the achievement.

Wallace might be small, but the downtown has been preserved enough to see just how big of a city it once was. Every building in the downtown core of Wallace has been added to the National Registry of Historic Places, so stopping in this small town is like stepping back in time. With tours of the mines, the downtown area and even tours of the brothels, spending a little time in Wallace can be a very educational experience.

If you are a fan of museums, we highly suggest checking out Wallace District Mining Museum & Visitor Center. Open Monday through Saturday in the months of April through October, this museum will answer any and all questions you may have on the city, the region and the culture of the town.

Wallace isn't just known for mining though. It is a great place for skiing, hunting, zip-lining and hiking. Wallace even has ties to Hollywood, being both the birthplace of the star of the Silver Screen Lana Turner and the setting for the fictitious disaster movie, "Dante's Peak."

Do yourself a favor, stop in Wallace and explore some seriously awesome sights.

Directions: In Missoula, Montana, take the North Reserve Street at Exit 101 on Interstate 90. Drive south 4.5 miles to South Ave West and take a right. Take the first left to Old Fort Road and follow the signs to the fort.

Fees: None

Highlights: Historic Buildings, Scenic Views, Museums, Wildlife

Fun Fact: You can stage awesome pictures on the abandoned railroad tracks, like your favorite old-timey cartoon villain.

Fort Missoula Montana

Fort Missoula is what many consider to be the quintessential fort in Montana. Home to the famous Buffalo Soldiers, this fort was created to protect settlers from the possible threat of the local tribes who were demanding their land back. While not directly on the main road, the Fort Missoula complex is well worth the slight detour. With original buildings, museums and wildlife viewing, you will be pleased with the area.

Built in 1877, Fort Missoula currently holds 16 historic buildings, some original and some rebuilt. The rebuilt buildings include the Headquarters, the Post Exchange, a Quartermaster Storehouse, the Hospital, two Barracks and seven Officer's Quarters. The Quartermaster Storehouse building is now home to the Fort Missoula Historical Museum. The original fort buildings that can be seen include a Carriage House (built in 1880), a stone powder magazine (built in 1878) and restored Non-Commissioned Officer quarters, which were built in 1878.

While stopping here, have a picnic, explore the grounds and watch for falcons, rabbits, coyotes and fox as they are frequently seen in the region. Standing next to train cars and old buildings, Fort Missoula offers a chance to step back 150 years and see how life was during Montana's Settlement.

While here, please be respectful, as this was the location of not only bad blood between the natives and settlers, but was also an internment camp during WWII, housing not just Japanese Americans, but also German and Italians who were residents of America, as well as sailors taken as prisoners of war.

Directions: Take Exit 101 and turn left on Reserve Street. Continue north two blocks and turn left at the bronze elk.

Fees: None

Highlights: Huge elk, educational opportunities

Fun Fact: This location helps non-hunters understand why hunting is needed for maintaining the elk population.

Rocky Mountain Elk Foundation's Elk Country Visitor Center

If you love elk, this is the destination for you. Sure, the visitor center and Rocky Mountain Elk Foundation supports hunting, but that is not a reason for those of you who are against hunting not to stop here. With fun interactive exhibits that allow you to see, touch and hear elk, this destination is one of the more educational stops we encourage.

Complete with the most impressive display of trophy elk mounts, visitors are encouraged to take pictures, handle elk antlers and shop at the gorgeous gift shop, located by the front door. Take the short nature trail and look for white-tailed deer, bald eagles, turkeys, owls and a rare moose or elk.

With 22 acres to explore, the Rocky Mountain Elk Foundation's Elk Country Visitor Center is a fantastic spot to stretch your legs and start getting excited for wildlife viewing.

To best experience the area, we recommend signing up for a tour. You can sign up for a tour by emailing tours@rmef.org or calling 1-866-266-7750. Tours are only given 9:00 a.m. – 4:00 p.m. Monday – Friday.

Directions: Take Exit 194 on Interstate 90 in Montana. Follow the
signs to the city.

Fees: Variable

Highlights: History, Cars, Old West
Prison, Views, Awesome Summer
Sunsets

Fun Fact: Deer Lodge was the sight
of the College of Montana, the first
higher-learning institution in the
state, founded in 1878

Deer Lodge

According to the town website, "Deer Lodge, Montana is home to
more museums and historical collections than any other town in
the Northwest. There are 22 acres of history and nostalgia to cap-
tivate young and old alike. The Old Montana Prison including The
Frontier Museum along with the Powell County Museum will trans-
port you back to the era of cowboys and the Old West. The Montana Auto Museum with over 150 vehicles, and Yesterday's Playthings—Montana's foremost doll and toy museum, will entertain
"children" of all ages. Cottonwood City displays the Snowshoe
Creek School, Blood Cabin and other buildings."

Website talk aside, Deer Lodge is home to 3,000 Montanans, one
car museum and one Old West prison. Seriously, Deer Lodge is a
great historical city and well worth the stop. In fact, Deer Lodge
makes a great destination to stay the night, as it is close to Yellowstone and is one of the more western-feeling towns along this
stretch of Interstate 90.

Gold was discovered near Deer Lodge in 1862. Subsequent discoveries in Bannack and Virginia City prompted a gold rush that attracted men and women of both good and bad character. Thievery, lawlessness, and murder prevailed until vigilante groups organized and hung or banished many of the worst criminals. In the winter of 1866-67, the Territorial Legislature requested funds for a prison. The United States Congress quickly approved the request, but the funding was inadequate.

Deer Lodge was picked for the site of the new Territorial Prison. Funding problems caused many delays and revisions in the plans, but construction finally began in the spring of 1870 and the first wing was completed by fall of the same year. The first convict was received on July 2, 1871. On November 8, 1889, Montana became the 41st state and the burden of operating this prison fell on the shoulders of the new state government. Inadequate funding and overcrowded conditions have plagued this facility for over 100 years. In 1979, this prison was abandoned in favor of a new facility, five miles west of Deer Lodge.

Today, the Old Montana Prison is listed on the National Register of Historic Places and is preserved and operated as a museum by the Powell County Museum and Arts Foundation under a lease

With two main attractions, Deer Lodge can easily consume an entire afternoon. The highlight for most will probably be the Old Prison Museum at the site of the old Montana State Prison. Built in 1870, this old series of building is on the National Register of Historic Places. Built entirely by inmates of the Old Montana Prison, this turn-of-the-century prison looks like a huge fortress. Rumor has it that it was home to at least one member of Butch Cassidy's "Wild Bunch." There are guided and self-guided tours available that lead you through the original Cell House and into the slide bar cells and isolation rooms of maximum security.

If prisons aren't your thing, check out the Montana Auto museum, located right next to the Old Prison. With an awesome collection of cars, ranging from a replica of an 1886 Benz and an original 1903 Ford Model A Runabout to nearly every classic car you can imagine, the Auto Museum in this small town is beyond impressive. Even if you aren't that into cars, seeing the collection of over 150 cars will give you a new appreciation of just how far we have come in automobile styles, comfort levels and gadgetry. As you walk around looking at cars used to take the first visitors to Yellowstone, think of your road trip to Yellowstone and how significant such a drive used to be for the first guests.

While there is not much else is in town to see or do, Deer Lodge is a pretty rad stopping point. Being able to stretch your legs and take in both the Auto Museum and the Old Prison is a super fun experience that you don't want to pass up. Pose for pictures, dream of cars and embrace your inner outlaw in this small, historical town just a few hours from Missoula.

In fact, don't take our word; take the word of the town's website: "Whether your interest is in the famous or infamous, gun fighting or ranching, adult toys or children's playthings, the museums of Deer Lodge will capture your imagination."

Directions: Take Exit 278 on Interstate 90 in Montana. Follow the signs to the city or the State Park

Highlights: History, Lewis and Clark, Old Inn, Wildlife

Fun Fact: This area was important to early Native Americans trappers, traders and settlers. The Flathead, Bannock and Shoshoni tribes all competed for control of the area, as did the trappers and settlers in later years.

Three Forks, Montana

On July 28th, 1805, Lewis and Clark officially identified a spot near present day Three Forks, Montana as the headwater of the Missouri River. The park, which sits at the confluence of the Jefferson, Madison and Gallatin Rivers, is the first section of the mighty 2,300 mile long Missouri River. This National Historic Landmark is not only a must for fans of the Lewis and Clark Expedition, but is also great for history and wildlife.

Aside from the awesomeness of standing on the banks of one of America's largest rivers, the Three Forks region is home to phenomenal wildlife watching. With migratory birds, as well as antelope, foxes and deer commonly seen, taking time out of your car to breathe fresh air and look at animals is a great idea. Being able to stand in the same spot where, over 200 years ago, two of the most famous explorers in America stood is amazing, and is only $5.

After visiting Missouri Headwaters State Park, head into the town of Three Forks to be taken back in time. The downtown of Three Forks probably hasn't changed much in the last century, and that is a great thing. As the most significant building in town, the Sacajawea Hotel and Restaurant, was built in 1910 and looks brand new to this day. The three story pillared building is beyond elegant for not only this region, but for most of the country. If you can, stay here for the night and you won't be disappointed.

While there are many other interesting shops and a few small museums in town, seeing the Missouri Headwaters and the Sacajawea Hotel gives you a great feel for the region, history and culture of Three Forks. Use this small city to recharge your body and keep heading to Yellowstone, as you are only 110 miles from West Yellowstone!

Directions: Take Exit 305 on Interstate 90 in Montana. Turn right (south) on North 19th Ave. In 3.7 miles, turn left on West Kagy Blvd. Follow signs to the Museum of the Rockies.

Fees: Adults- $14   Kids (5-7)- $9.50 4 and Under- Free

Highlights: Dinosaurs, Dinosaurs, Dinosaurs, History, Culture, Pictures, Planetarium

Fun Fact: With your admission, you'll receive a non-transferable Museum admission sticker that gives you unlimited access to the Museum for two consecutive days

Museum of the Rockies

The Museum of the Rockies is one of two amazing museums in the greater Yellowstone Region. Located in Bozeman, this museum is a must stop. Not only is it home to one of the largest dinosaur collections in the world, it also has a collection of historical photography from Montana, Idaho, and Wyoming. A stop here is for anyone who loves history, dinosaurs and pictures. Read:: everyone.

The Museum of the Rockies (MOR) is a Federal Repository for fossils, all of which are considered part of the United States' national treasures. There are also more Tyrannosaurus Rex fossils in MOR than in anywhere else in the world, making this remote building a world class museum. Without getting too geeked-out on dinosaurs, this museum is super rad. According to the Museum's website, "Accredited by the American Association of Museums, MOR is one of just 776 museums to hold this distinction from the more than 17,500 museums nationwide. The Museum is a Smithsonian Affiliate and a Federal Repository for fossils."

MOR isn't just about dinosaurs. The museum also has permanent exhibits on regional and Native American history, as well as the "Explore Yellowstone: Children's Discovery Center" exhibit. In all honestly, the Native American history section of the museum could use some work, but that shouldn't detract you from coming here. Every exhibit in the museum is fantastic, educational and fun. The museum seems to encourage interaction, making it the perfect stop after a long day on the road.

Still want more? The Museum of the Rockies also houses a planetarium that has programs unlike anywhere else. In 2014, they have three separate programs, all fun, educational and visually appealing. If you love Imax movies about science and nature, you need to check out this place. What could be better than seeing dinosaurs, learning about the regional culture and history and ending with a rad movie about life, the universe and everything?

Directions: Take Exit 256 on Interstate 90 in Montana. Follow the
signs to South Highway 2 and follow it south for almost 8 miles until
you see the signs for Lewis and
Clark Caverns State Park. Take a
left and enter the park.

Fees: Summer $10 for Adults, $5
for Children over 5 and under 11
years old

Highlights: Caverns, Hiking, Picnic
Area, History and Educational Opportunities

Fun Fact: The oldest natural feature in the cave is over 200,000
years old

Lewis and Clark Caverns

Lewis and Clark Caverns are part of the Montana State Park system. Originally a National Monument, the caverns not only boast
amazing limestone caverns (complete with stalactites and stalagmites), but also 10 miles of hiking trails and a campground. While
the hiking around Lewis and Clark State Park is pretty cool, the
highlight is that the caverns and should not be missed. With numerous tours, some by candlelight, this is hands down the best,
most accessible cavern in Rockies.

Touted as kid friendly, taking a tour through Lewis and Clark Caverns will make even the oldest visitor feel young. Walking through
the caverns isn't some lousy walk through a small series of
caves; it is vanishing deep into a hillside and exploring concert
size rooms filled with stalactites and stalagmites. While the limestone inside could be more glamorous, the guides who lead the
daily tours make up for it.

ɔst
ร
left

hil-

a,

the

Every trip we have ever taken has included incredibly knowledgeable guides, many of which have been geology majors from
around the nation.

While many of the caves features are incredible, the highlight of
the tour is the Cathedral Room. Properly named, this room is de-
ceivingly huge. Terraces of dripping limestone stack on top of
each other, forming majestic columns of all shapes and sizes.
Getting here isn't for everyone though, as tours are around 2
miles long and require quite a bit of physical exertion. You can
do it, but be aware that you will be hunching over, scooting up
and squeezing though a few places. It is completely manage-
able, but be aware of your limits. If you have vision problems or
do not cope well in tight places, you might want to skip this destination.

Directions: Take Exit 274 on Interstate 90 in Montana. Turn Right on US-287 South for 45.8 miles. Turn right on MT-287 N/E Main and continue for 14 Miles to Virginia City.

Fees: None

Highlights: THE GREATEST OLD WEST TOWN!!!

Fun Fact: In 1961, the town and the surrounding area were designated a National Historic Landmark District

Virginia City , Montana

No other city in Montana is quite like Virginia City. Tucked away on a little-used highway in the greater Yellowstone Region, this old mining town is a perfect snapshot of life in the Old West. Founded after an 1863 gold strike, 13 miles away in Alder Gulch, Virginia City popped up on the map, serving all the nitty gritty activities that come in boom towns. Now mostly empty, the remaining residents of Virginia City have salvaged this one decrepit ghost town and turned it into a time machine, transporting visitors back in time to the late 1800s.

At one time the pride of Montana, Virginia City today still has all the old wooden buildings it once was famous for. While not possessing the level of entertainment it once had, Virginia City does have a few antique stores, but the real draw to the town is the buildings themselves.

Preserved in time, thanks to a nearly dead local economy, the buildings still appear in the exact same style as they have since they were built. Raised wooden sidewalks connect the buildings in one of the most authentic Old West towns you may ever see.

Considered an "Alive Ghost Town", this town of 162 people once boasted a population of 10,000 people in 1864 and was once the largest town in the Inland Northwest. With stagecoach rides, train tours to Nevada City, Montana and chances to try your luck at gold panning, taking a side trip to Virginia City gives you a chance to live out your dreams of being an Old West gold-panner. The city's website also rightfully claims that it has "people in historic period dress, demonstrating historic skills, [and] sharing old world techniques."

Taking a trip through Virginia City is a perfect way to complete your transformation into the Old West. Just 90 miles from Yellowstone National Park, a stop in Virginia City will make you wish you could take a horse and ride your way all the way to the park. Bring your hat, your chaps and your boots and experience the greatest old west town in Montana.

QUICK STOPS

While the previous chapter was full of side day trips, this section highlights those stops that can take anywhere from five minutes to a few hours. Most are located right off Interstate 90, a few are off the beaten path, but still heading toward West Yellowstone

The stops here include parks, museums, incredible views and bi-
zarre stores full of every knickknack souvenir one could possible
want. From historical mining districts to bars full of silver dollar
coins to visitor centers and bull testicle themed stores, there is
something for everyone on this road trip. Starting with the Wild
Horse Monument in Washington State and ending with either
Quake Lake or the World Mining Museum in Butte, Montana (depending on your route), these stops will make the 755 miles to
Yellowstone National Park fly by.

WILD HORSES MONUMENT

Directions: Exit 139 on Interstate 90. Follow signs

Stopping here on a sunny day along the Columbia River is one of those truly must-do road trip moments. Just a few hours from Seattle, hiking to the metal horses placed upon the top of a ridge, overlooking the Columbia River is the perfect way to step out of Western Washington and into the "Old West." The hike is about a mile round trip and a little steep, but is 100% worth it. Bring a camera to pose for the first of many group shots and selfies.

Highlight: Catching this spot at sunrise or sunset.

Thorp Fruit and Antique Mall

Directions: Exit 101 on Interstate 90 in Washington State.

Eastern Washington is full of fruit stands, peddling their fantastic deliciousness every few miles. Many will be enticing, but one stands a little bit above the others on Interstate 90. The Thorp Fruit and Antique Mall is full of awesomeness, both in sight and taste. With free samples of candy, fruit and seasonal delights, a quick step into this two story building will provide some memorable snack items.

Highlight: The upstairs collectibles and antiques. Also, FREE SAMPLES!

Old Mission State Park, North Idaho

Directions: Take Exit 39 toward Old Mission State Park on Interstate 90 in Idaho.

Originally built in 1848, the Mission of the Sacred Heart has quite an amazing history. This church was built with local wood and supplied fabrics bought from the Hudson's Bay Company. It was placed here to convert the Coeur d'Alene Tribe. Pierre-Jean De Smet, the man who helped negotiate a treaty with Sitting Bull's Sioux and the US government, led the first expedition to the region in 1842. The building itself is super pretty, but knowing that this building's residents were handing out small-pox blankets to the Natives really tarnishes the image. Stop here and be respectful, as it is a huge piece of America's history, showing the negatives of the "Old West."

Highlight: Mission of the Sacred Heart is the oldest standing building in Idaho.

50,000 Silver Dollar Bar

Directions: Exit 16 on Interstate 90 in Montana.

No road trip is complete without a moment that will leave you speechless and the 50,000 Silver Dollar Bar is that place. It isn't pretty. It isn't natural. By no means is it scenic. This place is Wall Drug's second cousin. While the main draw to this stop is a bar and barroom embedded with 50,000 silver dollars, the shopping opportunities of this restaurant, bar and casino are reason alone to stop. With nearly everything that was made in China with the word "Montana" on it, the store is a window-shoppers dream. From clothes to swords, to fake cats in nests, wood carved knickknacks and suits of armor, you will find a gift for anyone here. If for nothing else, stop here to get gas, use the restroom and take a quick browse. You probably won't regret it.

Highlight: This store. It is mind-numbing and amazingly interesting. Well worth a stop.

St. Regis Travel Center

Directions: Exit 33 on Interstate 90 in Montana. Follow signs to Old US Highway 10. At the stop sign turn left. You will see the building.

If you like visitor centers where you can see trout in an aquarium as well as taste of one the best huckleberry pies on I-90, than this is the stop for you. The center offers free popcorn to everyone and a nice little gift shop that feel welcoming. The ice cream is delicious and the staff's knowledge is outstanding, but the best feature of the St. Regis travel center is watching the trout swim in the aquarium. Check out the huckleberry gifts, as they are all awesome.

Highlight: Watching live trout swim while munching on popcorn and pie.

Testicle Festival and Rock Creek Lodge

Directions: Take Exit 126 on Interstate 90 in Montana. Follow the signs and head toward the only buildings visible (To your South East)

Every road trip needs an interesting food experience, and the city of Clinton, Montana offers a glimpse into the silliness that comes from cattle ranching. You can get typical greasy fare in the restaurant, and you can also try deep-fried cattle testicles, called Rocky Mountain Oysters. Best with hot sauce and an inactive imagination, trying these will help you get in touch with your inner Old-West adventurer. Even if you don't try the Rocky Mountain Oysters, stop for a silly t-shirt, mug, or keychain.

Highlight: Being in town during the Testicle Festival, held:

2014 July 30th - Aug 3rd

2015 July 29th - Aug 2nd

2016 Aug 3rd - 7th

2017: Aug 2nd - 6th

Madison Buffalo Jump State Park

Directions: Exit 283 on Interstate 90 in Montana. Head south on Buffalo Jump Road and follow the signs to the destination.

Madison Buffalo Jump State Park is an awesome place to explore and contemplate how life was lived before guns and horses. A huge limestone cliff situated on the edge of a wide valley, this site was an amazing hunting ground for nearly 2,000 years. It wasn't that they hunted here that makes it awesome; it was how they did it. Dressed in wolf pelts, the Native peoples stampeded vast herds of bison off this massive semicircular ridge. Women and children waited below, ready to skin, clean, and prepare the buffalo meat and prepare the hides for clothing and blankets. While it is hard to image what the scene must have looked like, the park does a good job trying. With visible bones, awesome displays and gorgeous scenery, stopping here is one of the more wise choices you can make.

Highlight: Using your imagination to see herds of bison plummet off the cliffs to support the cycle of life.

The City of Butte and The World Museum of Mining

Directions: From Seattle, take Exit 124 on Interstate 90 in Montana. Keep right at the fork and head toward South Excelsior Avenue. Turn left onto South Excelsior Avenue. At 9/10ths of a mile, turn left on West Park Street. In 7/10ths of a mile, turn left on Mining Museum Road.

Butte is the butt of many jokes; the fact that many consider it an ugly mining town with a huge, smelly hole in the middle of town doesn't help. Butte, for what it lacks in beauty more than makes up for in history and understanding just how rough life can be in the middle of Montana. Located on the western edge of the Continental Divide, Butte has a great historical district known as "Uptown Butte" and is home to over 4000 historic buildings. It is just one of two entire cities to be named a National Historic Landmark. The World Museum of Mining exhibits are also quite interesting, even for those who hate seeing how horrible humans can be to the earth.

Highlight: The World Museum of Mining. With 66 exhibits, including a walkable town and a fake mine, it can't be missed. Also, you can take an underground mine tour.

Our Lady of the Rockies

Directions: Exit 129 on Interstate 90 in Montana. Merge onto Interstate 15 toward Helena. Take Exit 134 toward Woodville. Turn right toward X-L Heights Road. Take another right on X-L Heights Road. Follow X-L Heights Road for 4.6 miles then turn right on an unnamed road for 1.6 miles to destination

Normally, taking a detour such as this along a dirt road would be something we would advise against, but once you see the huge statue looking over the city of Butte, you will be glad we gave you information on this region. Built from 1979 to 1985, this 90 foot tall statue sits on the Continental Divide. While appearing to be a Catholic statue, the builders claim it is completely non-denominational. While standing next to the statue is obviously the main draw, taking in the views from the ridge can be quite impressive. Looking down into the city of Butte, one can easily see scars from mining. Looking away from the city, the term "Big Sky' is fully comprehended.

Highlight: Views of the mines of Butte from high above.

Island Park

Directions: Exit 256 on Interstate 90 in Montana. Follow signs for Montana Highway 2. Drive 14 miles until you come to US Highway 287, where you will head south. Stay on US 287 for 68.4 miles. Turn right on Montana Highway 87 South, which becomes Idaho Highway 87 South. Turn right on Highway 20 West and follow the signs to Island Park, Idaho.

This destination is quite out of the way, but is super unique and quirky. Home to the World's Largest Main Street, Island Park, Idaho is one of those quirky places that could only exist because of ridiculous liquor laws. At 15 miles long, this "city" was created to get around the Idaho laws that prohibit sales of liquor outside city limits. Local lodge owners and resort operators voted for incorporation, making the entire region one town. The official population is just under 300 people, making this town one of the least crowded cities in the world. While there is little to see or do in the town, it is worth driving along just to say you did it.

Highlight: Knowing that if you have three people in your car, you have the equivalent of 1% of the town's population with you.

Quake Lake

Directions: Exit 256 on Interstate 90 in Montana. Head toward State Route 359 toward Cardwell/ Boulder. Turn right on Montana Highway 2 East for 14.7 miles. At US Highway 287 South, turn right. Follow the signs to stay on US Highway 287 South until you reach Quake Lake after driving for 74.1 miles.

Located in southwestern Montana, Quake Lake was formed on August 17th, 1959, when an earthquake, measuring 7.5 on the Richter scale, hit the region. The quake caused an 80 million ton landslide that blocked the Madison River, killing 28 people who were camping along the banks of the river. While less noticeable today, the impact of this quake can still be seen. A visible scar on the mountains and a huge debris field are visible from the road. A visitor center exists on top of a ridge overlooking the damage, but it is hardly worth the price they charge for admission. If you are interested in this, you need to stop here to learn more. If you just want the background info, our description should suffice.

Highlight: Seeing the sheer power of a landslide and seeing a lake that didn't exist 60 years ago.

WHICH YELLOWSTONE ENTRANCE?

Inevitably, you must make important decisions on any road trip, and deciding which gate to enter Yellowstone is huge. Picking the right gate not only has the ability to dictate your daily itinerary, but can also be the difference between a good trip and a great trip. Luckily, we can help you make the right choice.

Choosing between West Yellowstone to the west (duh) and Gardiner to the north is broken down into three main factors. For a more detailed description of Gardiner and West Yellowstone, as well as the other neighboring cities, please turn to Trips Outside of the Park starting on page 191.

If you were hoping to decide which city to drive to based on estimated driving time and distance, we have bad news. With both entrances, it takes about 12 hours from Seattle. Gardiner is longer, by 14 miles. Choose wisely, but don't worry too much, both are amazing and beautiful in different ways.

WEST YELLOWSTONE

Distance from Seattle: 739 Miles

If you are heading to West Yellowstone, you will exit I-90 earlier, but you get a chance to see Virginia City, Quake Lake, and a few other hidden gems along the route. This route is much more quaint, as you drive through huge fields full of cattle, antelope and deer. The drive to West Yellowstone really helps you feel you are getting far off the beaten path and you are bound to see more antelope, hawks and birds along the way. The roads can be less crowded, the air seems a little crisper and the pace of life, as well as the speed limit, is a little slower. That is, until you get to the city of West Yellowstone.

Around major warm weather holidays and the month of August, West Yellowstone is a bit more hectic. With an Education Center/Zoo, an IMAX theater, a McDonalds and a railroad museum, it is quite the draw. With ice cream, touristy activities, and a great amount of local history, entering the park through West Yellowstone kicks off your trip in a fun, energetic way.

A more jaded traveler would say that West Yellowstone is the Reno of the National Parks. While obviously an exaggeration, there is a lot of truth to this statement. The town of West Yellowstone may only have a population of around 1,300 people over 512 acres (roughly over 2.5 people per 43,560 sq. ft) but it can appear much more crowded than that. Around major warm weather holidays and the month of August, West Yellowstone is a bit more hectic. With an Education Center/Zoo, an IMAX theater, a McDonalds and a railroad museum, it is quite the draw. With ice cream, touristy activities, and a great amount of local history, entering the park through West Yellowstone kicks off your trip in a fun, energetic way.

Fall is the best season to enter the park through West Yellowstone. The male elk, which are in rut, will challenge each other, both physically and verbally, their bugles heard over the usually misty Madison River. In the summer, osprey, elk a few bison and a rare bear can be seen wandering in the river valley alongside the road. This is also the fastest way to get to Old Faithful and the majority of the thermal features.

GARDINER, MONTANA

Distance from Seattle: 754 Miles

The road to Gardiner is by far the most direct route to Yellowstone, with only one turn off of Interstate 90 before the park entrance. While it is simple to get to, this area is beautiful and gives quite an historic journey on your way to town. Once in Gardiner, the views get even better, as you get to enter the park from the famous Yellowstone Arch, the official entrance to the National Park.

The road to Gardiner is considered by many to be pretty uneventful, but does allow a stop in the small town of Livingston, Montana. This stop has some decent gift shops, as well as a Subway and an Albertsons. Livingston also has quite a few fly-fishing stores, so if you are into some awesome fishing, a stop here is much needed. Livingston is basically a truck stop of a town that is now growing into a tourist-friendly-zone. Pick up supplies here and head south toward Gardiner.

To an untrained eye, the road to Gardiner is not exciting. For many, it is a two-lane highway next to a river and some mountains. For most road trippers, it is the start of the adventure; the journey back in time to how the West used to be. We almost guarantee you will see an elk, deer or a bear along Highway 89. The drive to Gardiner from Livingston is where life starts to slow down from the high speeds of Interstate 90.

Weaving along the Yellowstone River, watch for signs of an old railroad track that once connected Yellow-stone National Park's north entrance to rail travel. In the early 1900s train brought scores of tourists down this valley to Cinnabar, Montana, located just a few miles northwest of present day Gardiner. From Cinna-bar, they would take horse drawn coaches to get to the entrance of Yellowstone National Park.

Gardiner today is pretty straight forward, as Highway 89 goes right through this small town of less than 1,000 people who call it home year round. With great little shops, whitewater rafting opportunities and resident elk wandering through town, this city is a fun stop. The raised, wooden sidewalks really make Gardiner feel like an Old West town. Situated almost directly on the 45th parallel, Gardiner is located half-way between the Equator and the North Pole, but that isn't even close to the main draw.

As you leave Gardiner, Highway 89 heads to the draw of the region, the Yellowstone Arch. The symbol of the National Parks, the Yellowstone Arch is visible for over two miles and was dedicated by President Theodore Roosevelt in 1903. The National Park creed "For the Benefit and Enjoyment of the People" is carved into the arch. This is the spot where Yellowstone truly begins.

Crossing under the arch is a rite of passage. Pose here for pictures and get ready for your Yellowstone vacation to officially begin. Soon, you will be at Mammoth Hot Springs.

WELCOME TO YELLOWSTONE NATIONAL PARK!

The journey was long, possibly emotional and more than likely, a bit longer than you would have liked. Forget the pain of the the long drive and get ready to celebrate because you are now at our nation's first National Park. Besides the honor of being the first National Park, the Yellowstone region is designated as both a World Heritage Site and Biosphere Reserve. Yellowstone covers 3,472 square miles and is home to the largest, high alpine lake in America, While it is best known for geysers, it is also home to incredible hiking, great fishing and some of the last remaining prairies in the nation. With so much to see or do, we will walk you through what we consider the most important information, the best locations and the places to make your trip to Yellowstone as close to perfection as possible.

Common Yellowstone Questions

Why is the park the way it is?

Yellowstone isn't just a volcano, it is a super volcano. The geysers, hot springs, and other thermal features of the area are here because the majority of the park sits on a caldera (a crater of a large volcano). Earthquakes are common -around 2,000 each year-, but generally smaller than a 4.0 on the Richter scale. Few of them are felt by visitors. At the time of publication, geologists have assured the public we are not at risk for another eruption. Animals are prevalent in this area mainly because of conservation efforts by the National Park Service. Proof of this can be seen in the thriving populations of the grizzly bear, the reintroduction of the gray wolf and a sustainable bison population. The bison in Yellowstone are the only bison in the world with original DNA from before the European conquest.

Why is it called Yellowstone?

The simple answer is that the sulfur of the area helped turn the rocks into a yellowish color. The long answer is much more interesting. In the 1800s, French trappers named the river "Roche Jaune," which is considered by linguists at Utah State University to be a translation of the Minnetaree Tribes name for the region of "Mitsiadazi", translating to "Rock Yellow River." American mountain men later translated the French name to English as "Yellow Stone."

When Did Yellowstone Get Discovered?

While Native Americans used the park for 11,000 years, most consider the discovery of Yellowstone to be when the first Europeans discovered it in 1808. John Coulter, a former member of the Lewis and Clark Expedition became a trapper in the area, but his claims to the region were not accepted until 1869, when the US sent their first expedition into the area, led by Jim Bridger. The first pictures of Yellowstone were seen in America's newspapers 1871 and within a year of the pictures being published, the region became a National Park.

Why was it made into a National Park?

While this subject could be an entire book in itself, the short story is that nearly everyone who had visited or heard of the area realized it needed to be protected and controlled by the government. Cornelious Hedges, a writer and lawyer from Montana, was a leader in National Park designation. Hedges wrote numerous detailed articles about his experiences in the park in 1870 and 1871. He expressed a desire to set the land aside as a protected national park. Hedges wasn't the first person to express this desire, though his writing was instrumental in helping form the current park.

How bad were the 1988 Fires?

Starting out as 250 individual fires, seven main fires were responsible for 95% of the damage. Over 800,000 acres of land burned, nearly consuming the historic Old Faithful Inn. Anyone over 30 years old should remember seeing the coverage on TV. The fires were terrible, but two great things came out of the ashes. The first was that the National Park Service started allowing smaller fires to burn naturally in the park, which they weren't doing before the 1988 fire. The second good aspect of the fire was new trees and better animal viewing. The forests of Yellowstone were dense, but after the fire, the animals of Yellowstone (very few of which were killed by the fire) were easier to spot.

Yellowstone Quick Facts

Size: 3,472 square miles. (Larger than Delaware and Rhode Island combined)

Terrain of the Park: 5% of the park is water, 15% is grassland and 80% is forest.

Highs and Lows: The highest point: 11,358 feet (3,462 meters) at Eagle Peak, the lowest point: 5,282 feet (1,610 meters) at Reese Creek.

Record Low Temperature: -66 F (-54 C) at West Yellowstone in 1933.

Animals: 67 species of mammals live in Yellowstone, including one endangered species, the gray wolf.

Trees: Yellowstone features seven species of conifers, with the most common tree (80% of the forests) being the lodgepole pine.

Waterfalls: There are 290 waterfalls that are 15 feet or taller that flow year-round, the tallest being the Lower Falls of the Yellowstone River at 308 feet.

Volcano: The Yellowstone Volcanic Caldera measures 45 miles by 30 miles in size and is home to around 2000 earthquakes a year and over 10,000 thermal features.

Archeology: There are nearly 1,600 archeological sites in the park.

Yellowstone Lake: The lake covers 131.7 square miles, with a maximum depth of 410 feet and an average depth of 140 feet.

Employees: There are 780 National Park Service employees, 400 of which are year-round. During the summer season, there are over 3,000 seasonal employees who run the concessions at the park.

Visitor Centers and Museums: There are nine visitor centers and museums throughout the park.

Hiking: There are over 1,000 miles of backcountry trails with 92 trailheads and 301 backcountry campsites. There are also 15 miles of boardwalks and 13 self-guided trails.

Guns: Guns are allowed in the National Park but are not needed. Even if you are backcountry camping, a gun isn't going to do much good. Leave it at home, as you have a better chance of shooting someone or yourself than needing it for protection from two or four legged animals. In 2013, a three year old girl accidentally shot herself in the head, dying instantly in the Grant Village Campground. She died because, according to witnesses at the scene, her parents were told by their friends that they needed protection from bears and wolves. Be smart, be safe and leave it at home.

National Park Etiquette

With the increase in interest in our public lands, we need to address an issue that has become more prominent in Yellowstone National Park. Over three million visitors arrive at the park each year and the level of speeding, road rage, bad driving and general rudeness along boardwalks, in shops and across the park has become common. From seeing cars chase bison down the road to people throwing their garbage along trails, the level of respect for nature seems to have waned. We are sure you will follow these tips, but please remind those around you to do the same.

Proper Etiquette on Trails

Besides being prepared (which we cover in our hiking section), there are a few things all hikers need to do. You should:

A) Always stay on trail

B) Be aware of animals

C) Pack out everything you pack in

D) Say hello to fellow hikers

E) Downhill hikers have the right of way

Proper Etiquette on Roads

You will probably notice that many drivers in Yellowstone give their entire state a bad reputation. California, Texas and Florida, this includes *you*. Driving in the National Park is an honor and a privilege, so be patient, calm and respectful of other drivers and the animals of the park.

A) **Observe the speed limit.** Speeding will result in a huge ticket, a bad accident or possibly you killing an animal.

B) **Be patient.** If you are stuck in traffic, it is probably for a wolf, bear or bison jam. Honking and trying to pass people accomplishes nothing, except making you look like an idiot.

C) **Use pull-outs.** If a car is right up on your bumper because you are looking for animals or enjoying your day, pull off at the first opportunity. Ignore them and keep having an awesome day. Also, do not create your own pull-out areas!

D) **Respect the animals.** If an animal is in the middle of the road, blocking your way, wait for it to leave on its own time. Do not honk your horn!

E) **Stay safe.** If an animal is on the side of the road, stay in your car unless you are at a safe distance and have pulled your car to an approved pull-off spot.

Proper Etiquette in Campgrounds

If you are camping in a designated campground, chances are you will be near quite a few other people. Remember to be respectful, quiet and keep your camp clean. Camping in these regions is a privilege, so be respectful.

A) **Leave all food in your car or in bear boxes.** Food can attract animals into camp. If animals like bears become used to the smell and taste of food, they will frequent campsites more often and eventually get relocated or killed for being too close to humans. Save a bear, put your food in the proper areas.

B) **Conceal everything.** If you are leaving for the day, put away your food, chairs, and laundry lines. The smells can attract animals and the wires can get tangled in elk antlers. When you leave, the only thing visible in your site should be your tent.

C) **Clean up.** Use only designated waste areas to clean dishes, throw out garbage or use the bathroom. Signs are posted in approved areas and rangers or campground hosts can direct you to the proper area.

D) **Observe quiet hours.** Each campground will have quiet hours that need to be observed. Do not ruin everyone else's trip by yelling to each other in the middle of the night or letting your car idle while it warms up early in the morning. Be conscientious and assume everyone else is an incredibly light sleeper.

E) **Be friendly!** Get to know the campground hosts and neighbors. If you are staying at a campsite in the park, chances are there will be a campground host. Get to know them, as they can tell you about animal sightings, great day trips and even give you a heads up on the weather. Talk to your neighbors as well, as you already have something in common: Yellowstone!

Etiquette with Animals

Wildlife can be found everywhere in Yellowstone National Park. In fact, very few people have taken a trip to the park without seeing at least one wild animal.

A) **The animals are not tame.** This should be common sense, but you will see people running toward a bear to take pictures, so be prepared. Animals can and will attack you, but the odds are, it won't be a bear. More people are attacked by bison and elk than any other animal in Yellowstone. Bison can run 30 miles an hour for quite a while, much faster than you.

B) **Keep proper distance from animals.** For bears and wolves, you are required to stay at least 100 yards away, but rangers may enforce an even stricter limit. For all other animals, the rule states you need to stay at least 25 yards away.

C) **Be quiet and still around animals.** If you are watching an animal in the wild, or even at a zoo, you should always be as quiet as possible. Do not yell, talk loudly or wave your arms wildly. Try to blend in with your surroundings as best as can and remind others around you to do the same.

D) **Keep your dog in your car, or at home.** Yellowstone is not pet friendly, and nothing is more frustrating than seeing someone walk their dog up a ridge to get a closer view of an animal. This is not only against park policy, but it also may keep animals away from that region for a long time.

E) **Don't spook the animals!** If you must drive past an animal in or near the road, please do so as slowly and safely as possible. Do not try to scare the animal off the road by speeding up, revving your engine, or honking your horn, all of which are things we see each year when go to Yellowstone.

Etiquette for Pull-Off Spots

With hundreds of places to watch for animals, take in the view or just let an impatient driver pass you, Yellowstone's pull-off spots can get quite crowded, especially if there are animals nearby.

A) **Respect the onlookers!** If you see a crowded pull-off spot with numerous people using or standing near spotting scopes and binoculars, stop and ask what they see. Chances are, they are either waiting for something awesome or see something awesome. Be aware that there are groups of locals who will be rude to you and say they haven't seen anything, when they have. Always stick around and talk to more than one person.

B) **Share your experience.** If you spot an animal and someone asks what you see, tell them. Don't keep animals a secret. We are all here to enjoy the park and to experience nature. Share the experience and follow the golden rule.

C) **Park responsibility.** Do not double park or block people in. While this seems logical, the excitement of seeing a bear or a wolf will cause all logic to fail. If your car doesn't fit in a parking spot, leave the spot open for someone else to take and find someplace else to park. If the pull-off spot is full, drive to the next one down the road and walk. You can let everyone else jump out of the car though!

D) **Use only approved pull-off spots.** While you might be tempted to inch your way off the road to be closer to a wildlife viewing opportunity, driving off the road severely damages the ground. Creating your own pull-off spot is a slippery slope and needs to be stopped right away. Trust us, you will see some creative off-road parking if a wolf or grizzly is around.

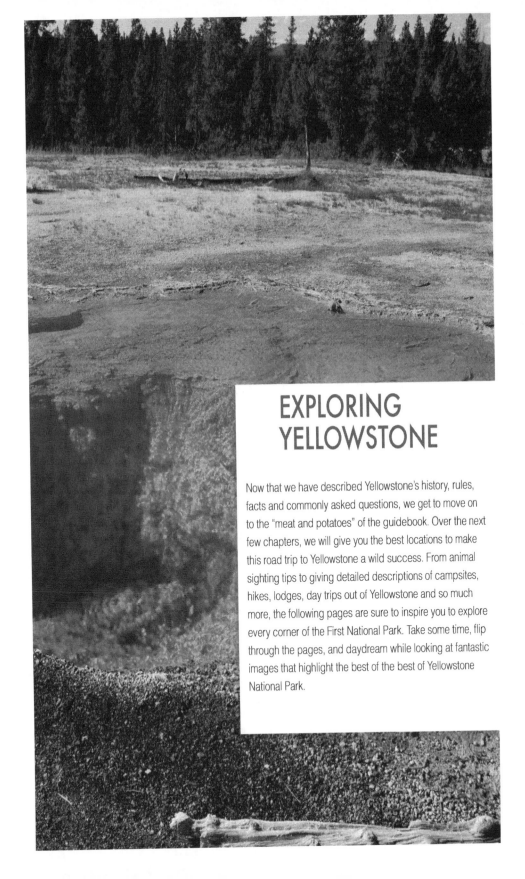

EXPLORING YELLOWSTONE

Now that we have described Yellowstone's history, rules, facts and commonly asked questions, we get to move on to the "meat and potatoes" of the guidebook. Over the next few chapters, we will give you the best locations to make this road trip to Yellowstone a wild success. From animal sighting tips to giving detailed descriptions of campsites, hikes, lodges, day trips out of Yellowstone and so much more, the following pages are sure to inspire you to explore every corner of the First National Park. Take some time, flip through the pages, and daydream while looking at fantastic images that highlight the best of the best of Yellowstone National Park.

THE ROADS OF YELLOWSTONE QUICK SHEET

There are 12 sections of road in Yellowstone you need to be familiar with to better understand the layout of Yellowstone National Park. With two main loop drives and five roads that lead to entrances, the roads of Yellowstone each offer their own unique highlights. There are 251 miles of total roads inside the park, so driving around can be quite a journey.

While this won't serve as a mile-by-mile guide to the park's road system, it will give you the quick facts about each region, hopefully helping you plan your visit.

West Yellowstone to Madison

Distance: 14 Miles

Best Time of Day: Morning or Evening

Best Season: Spring and Fall

Possible Animal Encounters: Elk, Deer, Big Horn Sheep, Bison

Highlights: Nice picnic spots on the Madison River

Hidden Awesomeness: Views of Mount Haynes

Madison to Norris

Distance: 14 Miles

Best Time of Day: Morning

Best Season: Spring and Fall

Probable Animal Encounters: Bison, Elk

Highlights: Monument Geyser Basin, Norris Geyser Basin

Hidden Awesomeness: Artist Paint Pots, Gibbon Falls

Madison to Old Faithful

Distance: 16 Miles

Best Time of Day: Morning

Best Season: Spring, Summer, Fall

Possible Animal Encounters: Bison, Coyotes

Highlights: Firehole Lake Drive, Midway Geyser Basin, Biscuit basin

Hidden Awesomeness: Swimming at Firehole Canyon Drive

Old Faithful to West Thumb

Distance: 17 Miles

Best Time of Day: Mid-day

Best Season: Spring

Possible Animal Encounters: Elk

Highlights: Crossing the Continental Divide Twice, Isa Lake

Hidden Awesomeness: Lone Star Geyser Hike

West Thumb to South Entrance

Distance: 22 Miles

Best Time of Day: Morning or evening

Best Season: Summer

Possible Animal Encounters: Elk

Highlights: Lewis Lake

Hidden Awesomeness: Moose Falls

West Thumb to Fishing Bridge

Distance: 21 Miles

Best Time of Day: Sunrise or sunset

Best Season: Summer

Possible Animal Encounters: Elk

Highlights: Driving along Yellowstone Lake

Hidden Awesomeness: Picnic on Gull Point Drive

Fishing Bridge to East Entrance

Distance: 27 Miles

Best Time of Day: Morning and Evening

Best Season: Spring and Fall

Possible Animal Encounters: Bear, Elk, Big Horn Sheep, Moose

Highlights: Sylvan Pass

Hidden Awesomeness: The views from Lake Butte Overlook

Canyon to Tower Falls

Distance: 19 Miles

Best Time of Day: Morning and Evening

Best Season: Spring, Summer, Fall

Possible Animal Encounters: Bear, Elk

Highlights: Washburn Overlook

Hidden Awesomeness: Chittenden Road and Mount Washburn

Fishing Bridge to Canyon

Distance: 16 Miles

Best Time of Day: Mornings and Evenings

Best Season: Spring, Summer, Fall

Possible Animal Encounters: Bison, Coyotes, Bears, Wolves, Elk

Highlights: Mud Volcano, Hayden Valley

Hidden Awesomeness: Standing on a ridge in Hayden Valley in the morning and evening, listening to wolves

Tower to Northeast Entrance

Distance: 29 Miles

Best Time of Day: Morning and Evening

Best Season: Spring, Summer, Fall, Winter

Possible Animal Encounters: Bear, Bison, Antelope, Elk, Wolves, Coyotes, Badgers, Bighorn Sheep, Deer

Canyon to Norris

Distance: 12 Miles

Best Time of Day: Any time

Best Season: Spring, Summer, Fall

Possible Animal Encounters: Elk, bear, Deer

Highlights: Virginia Cascade Drive

Highlights: Soda Butte, Lamar Valley, Little America

Hidden Awesomeness: Scanning Lamar Valley with a spotting scope or binoculars

Tower to Mammoth/North Entrance

Distance: 23 Miles

Best Time of Day: Any

Best Season: Spring, Fall, Summer, Winter

Possible Animal Encounters: Bear, Elk, Wolves, Moose, Bighorn Sheep

Highlights: Blacktail Plateau Drive, Undine Falls

Hidden Awesomeness: Petrified Tree (which isn't that awesome)

Mammoth to Norris

Distance: 21 Miles

Best Time of Day: Any

Best Season Spring, Summer, Fall, Winter

Possible Animal Encounters: Bison, Elk, Bighorn Sheep, Deer, Coyotes

Highlights: Roaring Mountain, Golden Gate

Hidden Awesomeness: Museum of the National Park Ranger

CELL PHONE AND WI-FI IN YELLOWSTONE NATIONAL PARK

While some carriers do have service in Yellowstone, it is best to assume you don't have service anywhere. If your service is supplied by one of the major carriers, you will have limited service around the Park's more popular areas, such as Old Faithful, Grant Village, Mammoth and Canyon. Service at the time of publication was sketchy at best, and while some want service added to the entire park, keep in mind you are visiting wilderness. Keep your cellphone out if you need pictures with it, but otherwise, unplug and enjoy the company you have.

The urge to use your phone may be tempting, but try to remember to stay in the moment and appreciate what is actually going on in front of you. Taking a picture of an animal or a geyser is great, but make sure you take a few minutes to just sit back with no electronics and enjoy it. Use your phones less and your eyes more! Plus, do you really want to be "that person" who is texting their way through an Old Faithful eruption at sunset?

If an emergency does occur, dialing 9-1-1 works almost anywhere in the park.

Wi-Fi in Yellowstone

Wi-Fi is available in Yellowstone National Park, for a fee at selected lodges. While you may feel you need Wi-Fi, we again stress unplugging from your electronics and enjoying the trip. If you do need Wi-Fi that is free, somewhat fast and dependable, leaving out the West gate and entering West Yellowstone is your best bet. There is free Wi-Fi at the McDonalds and you can get it to work from the parking lot.

For more specific area with wifi, please refer to our lodges section.

CAMPING IN YELLOWSTONE

With over 2,000 campsites spread throughout 12 campgrounds, Yellowstone National Park does a good job at creating unique camping experiences for nearly every style of camping. As one of the most popular camping destinations in the United States, Yellowstone's campgrounds are spread throughout the park. Some of the campgrounds take reservations, while others are first come, first served. Some campgrounds have showers and

and laundry; others have a vault toilet and nothing else. While the campgrounds may offer different amenities and activities, they all offer one thing: camping in one of the most spectacular locations in the world.

Camping in Yellowstone is what you make of it. Whether you are a first-time camper or someone needing isolation, Yellowstone National Park offers something for everyone. Even in the most crowded of campgrounds, nature is all around, with endless possibilities for adventure in every campground. While we want you to enjoy the campground you stay at, be aware that the best Yellowstone experiences happen outside of the campground. Use your camp as a base, but remember to go explore the entire region.

For Backcountry camping information, please refer to the Chapter titled: Hiking

PRIMITIVE CAMPING: PEBBLE CREEK

Location: Northeast

Elevation: 6,900 feet

Dates Open: June 15th to September 29th

Fee: $15 a night

Total Sites: 27

RV Sites: Yes

Amenities: Vault Toilet

Reservations: No

Ranger Led Talks: No

Highlights: Animals, Remoteness

Lowlights: Isolation

Best Spot: Tent Site 26

Worst Spot: Site 16 or 17

Why Pebble Creek?

Camping at Pebble Creek is not for everyone. It is remote with zero connection with the outside world, the people who try to camp at Pebble
Creek are more at home in the woods than they are at a crowded campground. With only 27 sites, you don't get much more remote car camping in the National Park than this.

Primitive Camping: Slough Creek

Location: Northeast Corner

Elevation: 6,250 feet

Dates Open: June 15th to October 7th

Fee: $15 a night

Total Sites: 23 sites

RV Sites: Yes

Amenities: Vault Toilets

Reservations: No

Ranger Led Talks: No

Highlights: Wolves, Bears, Remoteness

Lowlights: Rough Road to Campground

Best Spot: Site 24

Worst Spot: Site 14

Why Slough Creek?

Slough Creek is considered by many to be the most awesome campground in Yellowstone National Park. Situated far away from the main road and tucked deep in bear and wolf country, this is always the first site to fill up. With just 23 sites, all of which are pretty great, Slough Creek is the most sought after campground for those who are tired of the busy campground life in the villages. If you are traveling to experience nature, but don't want to backpack, Slough Creek will meet your needs.

PRIMITIVE CAMPING: INDIAN CREEK

Location: Northwest

Elevation:7,300 Feet

Fee: $15 a night

Dates Open: June 13th to September 8th

Total Sites: 75

RV Sites: Yes

Amenities: ADA Accessible Sites, Vault Toilets

Reservations: No

Ranger Led Talks: No

Highlights: Remote Camping in the Geyser Basin, Great Stargazing

Lowlights: Rarely Open or Available

Best Spot: Sites 1-12

Worst Spot: Site 7

Why Indian Creek?

Indian Creek is the most elusive campground in Yellowstone. While not the most popular, the limited seasonal access makes this a sought after destination. Located just South of Mammoth Hot Springs and situated in a pretty valley, this tree filled campground offers a reprieve from the "city life" of the Mammoth Campground.

PRIMITIVE CAMPING: LEWIS LAKE

Location: South

Elevation: 7,800 feet

Fee: $15 a night

Dates Open: June 15th to November 2nd

Total Sites: 85

RV Sites: Yes, less than 25'

Amenities: Vault Toilets

Reservations: No

Ranger Led Talks: No

Highlights:

Lowlights:

Best Spot: Site W-15

Worst Spot: Site A-25

Why Lewis Lake?

Located on a forested hill above the beautiful Lewis Lake, this campground can be either amazing or disappointing, depending on the season and who is camping near you. While every campground can be loud, Lewis Lake tends to always have the more rowdy campers. With no real rangers in the area, just a campground host typically located far from most sites, the serenity of the lake can be broken by yelling and drinking. When Lewis Lake has respectful campers, it gives you remote views and isolation from the crowded campground of Grant Village to the north.

CAMPGROUND VILLAGES: MAMMOTH

Location: North

Elevation: 6,200 feet

Fee: $20 a night

Dates Open: Year Round

Total Sites: 85

RV Friendly Sites: Yes

Amenities: ADA Accessible Sites, Flush toilets, generator use OK

Reservations: No

Ranger Led Talks: Yes

Highlights: Close to amazing thermal features

Lowlights: Can get loud

Best Spot: Site 49

Worst Spot: Site 71-83

Why Mammoth?

Camping in Mammoth is like nowhere else. Waking up to the smell of sulfur and the sight of elk seem routine in the spring and fall months, which are excellent things in Yellowstone. The campground, which sits within walking distance to the shops, museums and restaurants of Mammoth is extremely well-maintained and a great place to spend your first time camping. While it can get loud, as it sits next to the main road, Mammoth gives you hiking trails to some of the most impressive hot springs in the world. With a great location and access to numerous amenities, camping at Mammoth can be quite fun and comforting.

CAMPGROUND VILLAGES: MADISON

Location: West

Elevation: 6,800 feet

Fee: $21.50 a night

Dates Open: May 2nd to October 19th

Total Sites: 278

RV Sites: Yes

Amenities: ADA Accessible sites, Flush Toilets, Pay Showers, Dump Station, Generator use OK

Ranger Led Talks: Yes

Highlights: Watching elk in the rut, walking along the river, location

Lowlights: Can be loud and crowded

Best Spots: Sites 272 to 292

Worst Spot: Site 30

Why Madison?

If you want to camp near a gorgeous river and a geyser basin, Madison Campground is your destination. Just 14 miles from West Yellowstone and full of elk, bison and osprey fishing in the river, camping here is a sought after experience. Madison is one of the best spots to camp if you don't want to be extremely remote, but want to get away from the villages that some other campgrounds have. While it can get crowded, most people who stay at Madison truly appreciate nature.

CAMPGROUND VILLAGE: FISHING BRIDGE RV PARK

Location: Lake Region

Elevation: 7,500Feet

Fee: $47.75 a night

Dates Open: May 9th to September 29th

Total Sites: 325

RVs: ONLY

Amenities: Flush Toilets, Pay Showers, Laundry, Dump Station, Hookups, Generators OK.

Reservations: Yes

Ranger Led Talks: Yes

Highlights: Location and Bear Activity

Lowlights: Can get loud, only for RVs

Best Spot: Site E-39

Worst Spot: C-1

Why Fishing Bridge?

If you have an RV and want to camp along Yellowstone Lake, this should be your only destination. With a marina, fantastic views of the lake and most commonly known for bear activity, this campground is quite the perfect getaway. If you are traveling with an RV, be aware that this campground fills up quickly and is often full from June to September.

CAMPGROUND VILLAGE: NORRIS

Location: Central

Elevation: 7,500 feet

Fee: $20 a night

Dates Open: May 16th to September 29th

Total Sites: 100

RV Sites: Yes

Amenities: ADA Accessible Sites, Flush Toilets, Generator use OK

Reservations: No

Ranger Led Talks: Yes

Highlights: Animals, views

Lowlights: Limited number of sites with great views

Best Spot: Site 13 or Site 14

Worst Spot: Site 45

Why Norris?

If you love small creeks though lush meadows, frequented by deer, elk and the occasional bear, then Norris is for you. Located next to the Gibbon River and Solfatara Creek, this 100 site campground feels much more remote than it actually is. Norris Geyser basin is just a 10-minute walk from the campground, giving you great views and places to explore, all from camp.

CAMPGROUND VILLAGE: TOWER FALLS

Location: North Central

Elevation: 6,600 Feet

Fee: $15 a night

Dates Open: May 23rd to September 29th

Total Sites: 31

RV Sites: Yes, but under 30'

Amenities: Vault Toilets

Reservations: No

Ranger Led Talks: Yes

Highlights: Bears, Waterfalls

Lowlights: Traffic, Noise

Best Spot: Site 15

Worst Spot: Sites 1-10

Why Tower?

If you want to be next to a waterfall and close to bear country, Tower is an excellent choice. While not the most scenic, you can't beat this location. Close to wolves, bears, great hiking and the more scenic, non-geyser areas of Yellowstone, guests who stay at Tower tend to only want to stay at Tower every visit they take.

CAMPGROUND VILLAGE: CANYON

Location: Central

Elevation: 7,900 feet

Fee: $26 a night

Dates Open: May 30th to September 14th

Total Sites: 273

RV Sites: Yes

Amenities: ADA Accessible Sites, Flush Toilets, Pay Showers, Laundry, Dump Station, Generator use OK

Reservations: Yes

Ranger Led Talks: Yes

Highlights: Location, views

Lowlights: Always seems to be full, cold nights

Best Spot: Site 95

Worst Spot: Sites 1 and 2

Why Canyon?

Canyon is another campground that people either love or hate. It is an amazing location next to the impressive waterfalls of the Yellowstone River, and in close proximity to bear, bison and bighorn sheep. It is great for nature lovers. However, it is one of the larger campgrounds, so it is close to food, entertainment and the Canyon Lodge. If you want the best of both worlds, close to natural wonders and civilization, then Canyon is perfect for you.

CAMPGROUND VILLAGE: GRANT

Location: Central

Elevation: 7,800 feet

Fee: $26 a night

Dates Open: June 21st to September 21st

Total Sites: 430

RV Sites: Yes

Amenities: Ada Accessible Sites, Flush Toilets, Pay Showers with 2 showers free each night, Laundry, Dump Station, Generator use OK

Reservations: Yes

Ranger Led Talks: Yes

Highlights: Sites on Yellowstone Lake, Sunset, Elk

Lowlights: Sites not on the lake loops

Best Spot: Site 318

Worst Spot: Sites 1

Why Grant Village?

Grant Village is the best campground for those who like to sleep next to a lake. While there are sites without lake views, every site is within a few minutes of a walk to the beaches of Yellowstone Lake. During the summer months, Grant can seem crowded and overwhelming, but as you get toward your site, the crowds fade away and the beauty of the region takes over. During the fall, camp here and listen to elk bugle all night between rumbles of thunder and incoming flocks of geese.

CAMPGROUND VILLAGE: BRIDGE BAY

Location: Central

Elevation: 7,800 feet

Fee: $21.50 a night

Dates Open: May 23rd to September 1st

Total Sites: 432

RV Sites: Yes

Amenities: ADA Accessible sites, Flush Toilets, Pay Showers, Dump Station, Generator use OK

Reservations: Yes

Ranger Led Talks: Yes

Highlights: Location, views

Lowlights: Very few trees between campsites, little privacy

Best Spot: Site 448

Worst Spot: Site 64

Why Bridge Bay?

Bridge Bay isn't for everyone. Located next to the Lake Village and Yellowstone, animal sightings are few and far between in the campground and the views from your site are average. That being said, an average view in Yellowstone beats a decent view in a city any day of the week. With plenty of opportunities to explore around the lake, as well as being a short drive to Hayden Valley, staying at Bridge Bay can be the perfect place to sleep and watch the sun set over Yellowstone Lake.

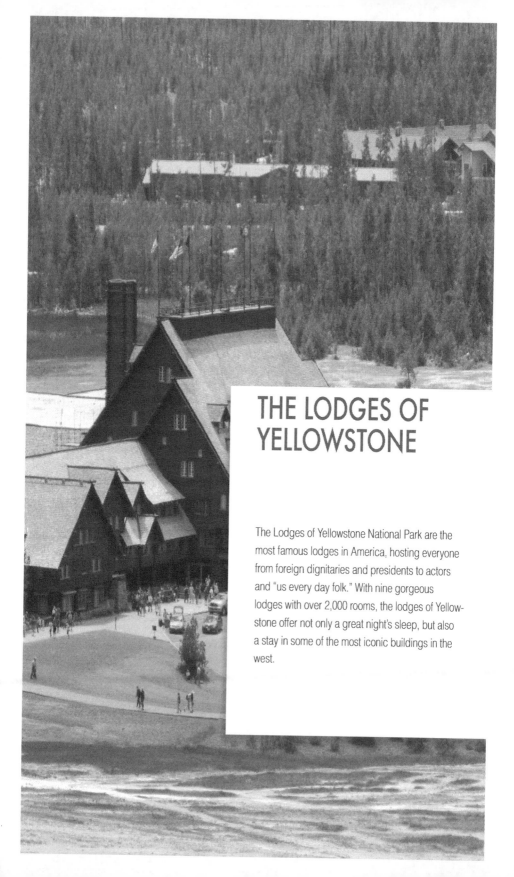

THE LODGES OF YELLOWSTONE

The Lodges of Yellowstone National Park are the most famous lodges in America, hosting everyone from foreign dignitaries and presidents to actors and "us every day folk." With nine gorgeous lodges with over 2,000 rooms, the lodges of Yellowstone offer not only a great night's sleep, but also a stay in some of the most iconic buildings in the west.

Each lodge is different and unique, but aside from one or two, they are all completely impressive and worth checking out. Even if staying in a lodge isn't your thing, taking a tour of Lake Hotel or the Old Faithful Inn provides amazing details about the history, culture and architecture of the region. The lodges are a must-see stop, and passing by these historical landmarks is a shame.

If you want to visit the lodges, but don't want to miss the prime animal viewing times, explore the old buildings around the heat of the day, when animals are the least active.

Bus Tours at Old Faithful Lodge

If you are too tired to drive around the park, you need to check out the Historic Yellow Bus Tours that run out of the old Old Faithful Inn. From sunset drives to photography tours, these open-top, bright-yellow buses are a can't miss, unique way to experience the roads of Yellowstone.

Be aware that they are on strict schedules and wildlife stops are minimal at best.

Mammoth Hot Springs Hotel and Cabins

Originally built in 1911, the hotel was upgraded in 1936 and is located on the site of Fort Yellowstone. Surrounded by hot springs, elk and military buildings from as early as 1886, the Mammoth Hotel still feels like it would be most comfortable having horse drawn carriages parked outside the front. While the hotel is pretty basic, the highlight of the structure, aside from the architecture, is the Map Room. The Map Room houses a gigantic wooden map of the United States, made from 15 different types of wood from nine countries.

The highlight of Mammoth Hot Springs would have to be their Hot Tub Cabins. While there are only four of them, the hot tub cabins come with a private, fenced-in hot tub that can accommodate up to six people. It also comes with a shower, toilet, sink and one queen bed. We're not sure what the park is trying to insinuate by giving one bed for a six-person hot tub, but it doesn't matter; these are the best places to stay. The other rooms are all fantastic, some of which are from the original hotel built in 1911.

Staying here gives you one of the most iconic Yellowstone experiences with an abundance of history, culture and a short walk to the world famous Mammoth Hot Springs,

Rooms: 97 rooms 104 cabins

Dates: Year Round

Internet: Only in Dining Room and Lounge for a fee of $5 to $25

Cost: $89 to $479 a night

Grant Village

Built in 1984, Grant Village is a nice place to stay on Yellowstone Lake. Named for President Ulysses S. Grant, the hotel is spread out over six separate two story buildings. As the closest lodge inside the park to the Grand Tetons, Grant Village is a great place for walks along the lake, elk watching and launching great day trips. Grant features a full service restaurant and a lounge. Staying here is nice, but there are better places to spend your money and experience the park.

Grant has yet to develop a true identity, as it more exists as a hotel than a lodge. If you love trees and lakes, this is a great spot; it just doesn't have the history of the other surrounding lodges. A stay at Grant will achieve three things. It will give you a nice place to sleep indoors, allow you close access to both Yellowstone and the Grant Teton National Parks and gives you a spectacular place to watch the sunrise on Yellowstone Lake.

Rooms: 300 rooms in six buildings

Dates: May to September

Internet: Wii-Fi in Public Areas for a fee of $5 to $25.

Cost: $155 a nigh**Canyon Lodge and Cabins**

.

If you have ever wanted to stay at a 1950's style lodge, Canyon is where you must go. It's décor is right out of your grandma's house, and it could have been the vacation destination of the Brady Bunch. While these may seem like negative things, Canyon most reminds us of how the 1950s were depicted in "Back to the Future." The architecture of the buildings is phenomenal, and while definitely stylized, it works perfectly for the location. Tucked away in the forest above the majestic falls of the Yellowstone River, this wooden lodge is well worth the stay.

With 81 rooms in two buildings, as well as 100 Western Cabins and 340 Frontier Cabins, it is easy to see why Canyon is so active. An entire village is spread out next to the cabins and lodge, complete with a museum, stores and a 1950's-style diner. The cabins and rooms are simple, but Canyon's location is what makes it so sought-after. Close to waterfalls and river, wolves, bear and bison, if you love exploring, you need to stay here.

Rooms: 81 rooms in two buildings. Dunraven and Cascade 100 west cabins and 340 frontiers

Dates: May to September

Internet: Wi-Fi in Public Areas for a fee of $5 to $25.

Cost: $99 to $194 a night

Old Faithful Inn

There are places to stay, and then there is the Old Faithful Inn. Built in 1903, this Inn is said by park officials to be the largest log structure in the world. The inn features a huge lobby built around the most massive, stone fireplace you have ever seen. Weighing 80 tons and standing 85 feet tall, this fireplace stands out in stark contrast to the deep colors of the exposed wood interior of the inn. A huge, hand-crafted clock rests on the fireplace, but you won't be concerned about the time of day here, much less the year.

The lodge is the 37th most popular building in America, according to a study by the American Institute of Architects and is extremely deserving to have been designated a National Historic Landmark in 1987. We could go on for pages about the inn. Stay here and take one of the FREE TOURS that are offered throughout the day. The history of this building is incredible and needs to be seen to be fully appreciated.

From suites to rooms with shared bathrooms, the inn has it all. While there isn't a bad room in the place, we have a favorite style of room. For us, the best rooms are the Old House Rooms. Built in 1904, the National Park hasn't changed décor from the original style. While rooms have been repaired, the styles are matched as best as they can. From color schemes and paintings to the original radiators still heating the room, these are the most historical rooms in the park.

Rooms: 329

Dates: May to October

Internet: None

Cost: $103 to $525 a night

Old Faithful Cabins

Built in 1920, the Old Faithful Cabins are some of the more affordable and enjoyable cabins in the park. Located close to the "city" of Old Faithful, They are within walking distance to the most impressive geological features in the world. If isolation is your thing, this location can be tough. However, staying here gives you endless opportunities to see Old Faithful and the neighboring geysers erupt at all hours of the night and day. Catch them at sunrise and sunset for a memorable view that few see.

There are two styles of cabins, the Frontier and the Budget. The Frontier Cabin has a shower, toilet, sink and either one double bed or one double bed and one single bed.

Budget Cabins are available and come with either one double bed and one single bed or two double beds. They also do not have a private bathroom or shower, but are substantially less expensive.

Rooms: 34 Cabins 100 Rooms

Dates: May to October

Internet: No

Cost: $74 to $124 a nigh

Old Faithful Snow Lodge

While this lodge was completed in 1999, the Snow Lodge fits in with the natural feel of the region. Built with heavy timber, the exterior of this lodge is made up of log columns and a cedar shingle roof. While the history and enormity may not be as great as the Old Faithful Lodge, the Snow Lodge is located along the boardwalk at Old Faithful, giving you 24 hour access to one of the natural wonders of the world. Comfortable, clean and home to four styles of rooms, staying here is a special treat for sure.

The four styles of rooms are Lodge Rooms, Western Cabins and Frontier Cabins. While mostly similar, the Lodge Rooms offer a few more every day amenities. Some say the Western Cabins are nicer, but the main difference between those and a Frontier Cabin, besides being more expensive is that they have two queen beds compared to the Frontier Cabins two twin beds.

Rooms: 96 cabins

Dates: Year Round

Internet: Wifi in Public Areas for a fee of $5 to $25.

Cost: $99 to $260 a night

Roosevelt Lodge

If you want a true Old West experience, a stay in the rustic cabins at Roosevelt Lodge is exactly what you need. Located on a ranch-like setting, complete with horse rides, stagecoaches and an Old West cookout (see food), the Roosevelt Lodge is named after President Theodore Roosevelt. President Roosevelt would frequent a campsite near the current site of the lodge on his hunting and nature watching trips. Rustic wooden cabins are tucked against hills, where one can spend an evening sitting on the porch in a handmade rocking chair, overlooking a valley frequented by elk, bison and bear. A stay at Roosevelt Lodge, built in 1920, is the ultimate Old West experience in Yellowstone, so if you are looking for somewhere to rock your Stetson and boots, this is the place.

The lodge features two types of cabins, we highly suggest staying here. Choose between the Frontier Cabin and the Roughrider Cabins to make your adventure perfect. The Frontier Cabin is simple, but offer beds, a shower a toilet and a sink. The Roughrider Cabins are less luxurious, but rad nonetheless. While they don't have bathrooms (communal showers and bathrooms are located nearby), they do have wood burning stoves for heat. Be aware that two free pesto logs are placed in your room daily, and burning your own wood is not allowed.

Rooms: 80

Dates: June to September

Internet: None

Cost: $74 to $124 a night

Lake Yellowstone Hotel

Originally built in 1891, this hotel became famous for its colonial style architecture, which was done during a remodel in 1903. Lake Hotel, as it is known by most everyone, is like stepping back into time. The three story complex looks more at home with horse drawn wagons parked next to it than it does with today's cars and RVs. Complete with huge columns and painted yellow, Lake Hotel sits right along the banks of Yellowstone Lake, contrasting beautifully against the greens of the trees and the blue of the lake and sky. With a sun room to enjoy the views without the common winds, staying at this lodge, which is on the National Register of Historic Places, is an incredibly awesome experience.

If the lodge isn't your thing, check out the frontier cabins, built in the 1920s. While duplex style, they offer two double beds, a private bathroom, a shower, as well as cool views.

Rooms: 304

Dates: May-October

Internet: Wired Internet

Best Room: Presidential Suite- three rooms, two bathrooms and a view that you will share with President Calvin Coolidge. Cost: $629 a night

Cost: $149 to $629 a night

YELLOWSTONE FOODS

If you are a foodie, Yellowstone doesn't offer much in the form of variety. With 11 restaurants and cafeterias in eight locations to pick up snacks or quick foods, you will never be too far from getting much needed nourishment; just don't expect amazing and regional fare. Don't be fooled: the food is good, it just could be so much better.

While not up to some people's culinary standards, the vast majority of us love the types of foods served around the park. From burgers and chicken strip to fries, milkshakes, salads steak and salmon, you can find tasty meals all around. While the majority of the foods aren't too expensive, they can cut into a budget quickly. If you are looking for a cheaper solution to food and while camping, try bringing foods to cook. Haven't you been looking for an excuse to eat hotdogs and s'mores all day anyway?

Best Unique Snack

When in doubt, pick up a package of elk or bison jerky from one of the General Stores spread throughout the park. The flavored licorice is also quite a tasty delight, especially the huckleberry flavor.

Best Ice Cream Stop

There are actually two locations where you can get the best ice cream. The first is the Bear Paw Deli near Old Faithful Inn and the other is at the Tower Visitor Center. While they won't have many flavors, there is something about ice cream and Yellowstone that fit together nicely.

Best Dining Hall

While Mammoth Dining Hall is great, eating at Canyon Village gives you great food with a much better atmosphere. Built in the 60s and 70s eating in Canyon gives two fantastic options. You can choose from the Canyon Lodge Cafeteria, which features a 1950s-diner-style fast food fare or walk next door to the Canyon Lodge Dining Room for an eating experience that has the same feel as the cafeteria, just classier.

Most Romantic Location

Nothing says romance in Yellowstone like dining at the Old Faithful Inn Dining Room. Get dressed up as best you can and have a classy dinner while watching the sun set over the geyser basin. The food selection is best here, but the atmosphere can seem a bit crowded and hectic. Ignore the distractions though and enjoy a nice glass of wine in a historical dining area.

Best Spot for Beer and Wine

With one of the best selections of wine and beer in Yellowstone, stopping off for an adult beverage in Mammoth needs to be added to your list. Domestic beers, microbrews, and mixed drinks, provide plenty of opportunity to overindulge. With over 45 wine options and 20 beers to choose from, if you are craving a drink, get it at Mammoth.

Most Kid-Friendly Location

The Lake Hotel Deli is the best option for kids, as they offer standard childhood favorites like PB&J, grilled cheese sandwiches, burgers, fries and pizza. The Bear Paw Deli, located near the Old Faithful Inn, is also great, as it serves burgers, grilled chicken fingers and ice cream.

Best Dining Experiences

The Roosevelt Chuck Wagon Dinner Ride is the greatest experience you can have while eating in Yellowstone. With songs, campfire stories and the possibility of seeing wildlife after riding on a stagecoach along Teddy Roosevelt's favorite spot in the park makes this trip one of the most memorable dining experiences you can have in the park.

YELLOWSTONE GIFT SHOPPING

No trip to Yellowstone is complete without checking out all the knickknacks in the gift shops. From sweatshirts and coon skin caps to books and plaster wolf prints, the stores of Yellowstone National Park have far more Yellowstone National Park kitsch than you probably think exists. While you may assume that the stores are all the same, each store carries unique goods that you probably won't see anywhere else. Some locations have outdoor stores, specializing in camping gear, spotting scopes and higher end fashion, while others may sell more educational toys, books and maps. While shopping in Yellowstone may seem like a waste, buying a souvenir becomes a tradition in itself.

For the best selection of books and educational shopping, you need to go to the Yellowstone Association Park stores, which are located at the major lodge areas. These are where you will find the best pictures, books and generally more wholesome gifts. If you are a nature lover, rest assured that your purchases are funding education opportunities for youth. The selection of gimmicky gifts may not be as large as other stores, but the goods they have are pretty rad. As an official partner of the Park Service, the Yellowstone Association helps with educational materials, road signs, and visitor center displays. Membership programs and sales through the stores also help fund research for the park.

The standard gift shops around the park are amazing in their own ways. While it is overwhelming to see 30 different styles "Yellowstone" t-shirts, it is amazing to think that a natural area is generating revenue based on the name itself. Yellowstone is not just a park, it is a brand, and nowhere is that more evident than in the gift shops spread throughout the scenic areas of the National Park. With nearly anything you can imagine for sale, browsing the gift shops is a great way to spend a rainy afternoon or beat the heat of the day. Most have snacks, some have ice cream, but all have something that will perfectly encapsulate your trip.

Yellowstone Association Stores

Located in Gardiner, Mammoth, Norris, Madison, Old Faithful, Grant, Fishing Bridge, Canyon, Lamar Buffalo Ranch, and West Thumb

Gardiner is the largest store and, at the time of publication the only store location that sells clothing.

There are also stores at the Bozeman Airport and inside the Quake Lake Visitor Center.

Yellowstone General Stores

Bridge Bay- Outdoor Store

Canyon- General Store, Outdoor Store, Gift Shop

Fishing Bridge- General Store

Grant Village- General Store, Mini-Store, Gift Shop

Lake- General Store, Gift Shops

Mammoth- General Store, Gift Shop

Old Faithful- General Stores, Gift Shops

Tower- General Store

Roosevelt- Mini-Store, Gift Shop

5 Shopping Tips for Yellowstone

1) **Expect disorganization.** These stores are not high end stores; they are busy tourist destinations at a National Park. Things will be out of place, they won't have certain sizes of clothes, aisles might be cluttered; life will go on.

2) **If you have it in your hand and you want it, buy it.** Not every store has the same gifts, and things can sell out very quickly. Case in point: I was going to buy my father a lanyard for his keys. There were 20 on the rack, but I decided I would return and grab one after I went to get a drink of water and use the restroom. When I returned a few minutes later, a woman was buying their entire stock of that lanyard. This has happened to me twice.

3) **The employees are not sales experts.** Many of the employees around Yellowstone are there for the summer, from all over the world. Be patient with them, be courteous and be friendly. Having worked here for a summer, I can tell you that nice customers always got better service.

4) **Watch your kids. If you have children, keep an eye on them.** There are hundreds of things to eat, throw, break and swallow. Kids will be kids, but also keep in mind that the stores are small and cramped, so make sure they are on their best behavior.

5) **Shop when you have nothing else to do.** The stores are open late for most of the summer, so do not miss out on Old Faithful, a stagecoach, a horseback ride or the chance to see wolves hunt elk because you are in a store. Yellowstone is a National Park for the beauty and uniqueness of the region, not because of their awesome stores.

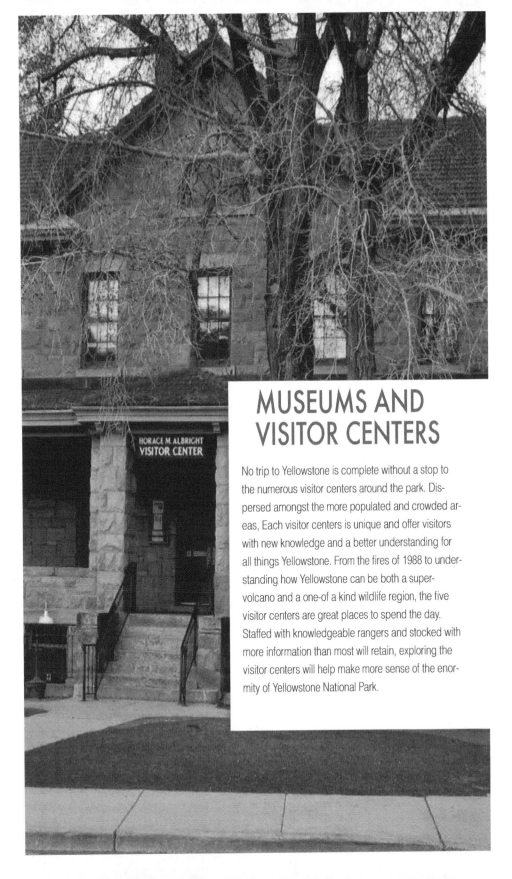

MUSEUMS AND VISITOR CENTERS

No trip to Yellowstone is complete without a stop to the numerous visitor centers around the park. Dispersed amongst the more populated and crowded areas, Each visitor centers is unique and offer visitors with new knowledge and a better understanding for all things Yellowstone. From the fires of 1988 to understanding how Yellowstone can be both a super-volcano and a one-of a kind wildlife region, the five visitor centers are great places to spend the day. Staffed with knowledgeable rangers and stocked with more information than most will retain, exploring the visitor centers will help make more sense of the enormity of Yellowstone National Park.

Grant Village Center

Open: Late May to Late September

Hours: 8am–7pm

While the lodge may seem stale and uninteresting, the Visitor Center focuses on the history of wildfires in the regions, as well and discusses modern-day fire management strategies. While on first glance that may not sound exciting, the main draw is an incredible display documenting and explaining the fires that tore through Yellowstone National Park in 1988. With 36% of the park being impacted by fires, Yellowstone National Park in 1988 was ablaze. This visitor center will give you fascinating exhibits, a great video and access to experienced rangers who can answer any question you can throw at them, including recent animal sightings.

Old Faithful Visitor Center

Open: April and May from 9am–6pm

May to October: 8am–8pm

October to November: 8am–4pm

If you have ever wanted to know the science and geology of the Geyser Basin of Yellowstone National Park, the visitor Center at Old Faithful offers a crash course for both geysers and girlsers of all ages. While you can tour this visitor center online, nothing compares to seeing the exhibits while standing a few hundred feet from Old Faithful. With hands on activities for visitors of all ages, this visitor center is perfect for all levels of education. If you have ever wanted to know about geysers, how they work and why they are at Yellowstone, explore the visitor center as you wait for Old Faithful to erupt.

Fishing Bridge Visitor Center

Open: Late May to Late September

Hours: 8am–7pm

If taxidermy of local animals is your thing, the Fishing Bridge Visitor Center has you covered. With a huge collection of stuffed birds, many will feel the need to avoid this visitor center, but those who do are missing out on an incredibly educational opportunity on birds and Yellowstone Lake. Built in 1931 the building is a National Historic Landmark because, it inspired "Parkitecture," the architecture so widely associated with National Park buildings across the country. Stopping by this visitor center gives a great appreciation for the avian visitors and life along the huge lake.

Canyon Visitor Center

Opens April to October

Hours: 9am–5pm

While the other visitor centers are nice, the Canyon Visitor Center is exactly what visitor centers are supposed to be. Describing the super volcano that is Yellowstone Park, Canyon is home to a visitor center that is quite time consuming. Start with an amazing film about the relationship between Yellowstone's geology and the wildlife in the area in a huge theater with comfy seats. After the show, check out the room-sized relief model of Yellowstone that shows past eruptions, lava flows, glacial activity and earthquake faults spread throughout the region. While the lower level narrates the park's eruptions, the second floor view of the model of the park is narrated through local tribe's history of the region. Besides those two awesome sights, there are numerous displays showing how large an eruption would be and giving more insight into how the park became the way it is, as well as a 9,000 pound rotating kugel ball that show the world's volcanic hotspots. If you need a few hours of educational awesomeness, this is where it is at. With the added bonus of a large information desk, staffed by Yellowstone experts, ask any and all questions regarding animal sightings, hikes, food or places to nap; they can answer any question!

Mammoth Visitor Center

Open: Daily and year-round

Spring Hours: May 9am–5pm

Summer Hours: Late May to Late September 8am–7pm

Fall and Winter Hours: October to May 9am–5pm

The main Mammoth Visitor Center is closed until May of 2015, but a temporary center is available. At the time of publication, the National Park Service had not released a list of exhibits that will be featured in the temporary exhibit. It will focus on the animals of the park.

The Mammoth Visitor Center is where you have to go if you want to see awesome exhibits about the local animals, the history of Mammoth and the history of art in Yellowstone National Park. This visitor center spotlights world class art and photography, as well as impressive taxidermy animals, a stop to the Mammoth Visitor Center will get you ready for the safari that you will be experiencing while driving the roads of Yellowstone. This is also a great place to ask about animal sightings throughout the park.

OTHER GREAT AREAS

Old Faithful Haynes Photo Shop

Hours vary seasonally.

Rebuilt along the boardwalk at Old Faithful, the Haynes Photo Shop was once the only place to get your pictures developed in Yellowstone National Park. Long before the days of digital cameras, this store once was the place to visit if you wanted to document your trip. Today, the store is a small museum, complete with amazing old pictures of Yellowstone, as well as an opportunity to pose for a free picture in front of an iconic Yellowstone background that gets sent to your email. As part of the Yellowstone Park Foundation, this building is great for fans of history, photography or really great, hands-on displays.

Museum of the National Park Ranger

Open: Late May to Late September

Hours: 9am–5pm

Located one mile north of Norris, this small museum highlights the history of the park ranger profession. With short videos and cool displays, this museum is a good stop if you need out of the car, or if you are really curious about the Rangers of National Parks. Informative and historical, take a few minutes to learn and appreciate all that Rangers do in our National Park System.

Junior Ranger Station at Madison

Open: Late May to September

Hours: 9am–6 pm

If you have or are a kid between the ages 5 and 12 years old, a stop at the Junior Ranger Station at Madison is a must! Here, you can pick up applications and a checklist to get your little guy or girl officially recognized as a Junior Ranger of Yellowstone National Park with an adorable patch. The 12 page application sounds tedious, but is actually great fun, giving your child a chance to really connect and learn about the park. Requirements to be a Junior Ranger include attending a Ranger-led program, hiking a park trail and learning about geology, wildlife and fire ecology. It is a blast and if you have a child make them do this!

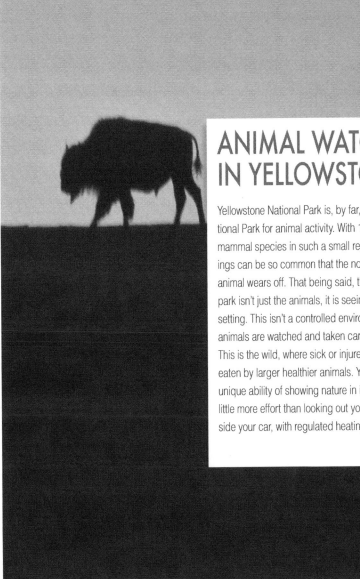

ANIMAL WATCHING IN YELLOWSTONE

Yellowstone National Park is, by far, the most active National Park for animal activity. With 12 different large mammal species in such a small region, animal sightings can be so common that the novelty of seeing an animal wears off. That being said, the highlight of the park isn't just the animals, it is seeing animals in a wild setting. This isn't a controlled environment, where sick animals are watched and taken care of.

This is the wild, where sick or injured animals get eaten by larger healthier animals. Yellowstone has the unique ability of showing nature in its truest form with little more effort than looking out your car window. Inside your car, with regulated heating and cooling and built to withstand incredible impacts, you can look through the automatic moving windows at a fox listening carefully for a mouse to eat or watch a grizzly bear eat the carcass of an elk. Wildlife watching in Yellowstone is quite an adventure, inside or outside of your car and we will help you make the best of however many days you have.

This is the wild, where sick or injured animals get eaten by larger healthier animals. Yellowstone has the unique ability of showing nature in its truest form with little more effort than looking out your car window. Inside your car, with regulated heating and cooling and built to withstand incredible impacts, you can look through the automatic moving windows at a fox listening carefully for a mouse to eat or watch a grizzly bear eat the carcass of an elk. Wildlife watching in Yellowstone is quite an adventure, inside or outside of your car and we will help you make the best of however many days you have.

There are three main ways to see wildlife in Yellowstone. Each offers similar animals, but the frequency of sightings may differ upon the environment. Whether you are watching from your car, watching from a spotting scope or watching while hiking, you should be able to see the majority of large animals in Yellowstone; it just depends on how dedicated you are to being at the right place at the right time. Following our insider tips below, your safari around Yellowstone will be one for the ages!

Obviously, we are aware that animals are wild and their behavior can't be predicted, but with years of observation, we have discovered a pattern that can be pretty reliable. Actually, it is something most people who travel to Yellowstone know, but now you can gain the knowledge without having to use all that gas. Finding animals in

Yellowstone is an all-day event, with good sightings being found all around the park. If you are wanting to see all the large mammals, be prepared for early mornings, late nights and a whole lot of time sitting in the car or standing on a ridge.

Car Watching

Rules

- **Do not pass or honk.** If vehicles around you are stopping or slowing down, but you can't see an animal, DO NOT PASS or HONK. Chances are there are some of the more rare animals up close, or a herd of bison decided to cause another "Bison Jam". Either way, honking and passing should not be done!

- **Bison Jams are common.** If your car is surrounded by bison, do not panic. Turn off your car, keep your hands and head in the car and sit back in awe.

- **Bear Jams are common**. If you come across a "Bear Jam", resist the urge to get out of your car unless it is safe. This rule may seem like common sense, but just wait, the things you will see...

- **Join the group.** If you see a group of cars pulled off, with everyone looking in one direction stop and see what they are looking at. Chances are, it will be something pretty cool, like a badger, fox, mountain goat or bighorn sheep.

IDENTIFYING TRAFFIC JAMS IN YELLOWSTONE

How to Identify Animals Based on Traffic

Good

If traffic increases, but there are only a few cars pulled out at the pull off areas, the animal will more than likely be an elk, a lone bison, an antelope, a badger or any of the numerous birds of the region.

Great

If traffic increases and it appears as if most of the pull-off spaces are being used, the animal will more than likely be an elk coyote, fox, bighorn sheep, or bison herd in the distance.

Best

If traffic has come to a standstill, with cars pulled off the road in every direction and people running ahead, the animal will more than likely be a black bear, a grizzly bear, moose, wolves or mis-identified coyote. There is also a high likelihood that it is a bison jam, especially if you are near Lamar or Hayden Valley.

ANIMALS ON THE ROADS: WHICH ANIMALS CAN BE SEEN ON WHAT ROADS?

Gardiner to Mammoth

Best Time: Any

The road from Gardiner to Mammoth is the one place where most visitors see bighorn sheep. Hanging out above the road, watch for these sheep jumping along the rocks cliffs. Other commonly seen animals in this region are Elk, Bison, Deer, and coyotes. While bear are occasionally seen here, they are quite rare and out of the ordinary.

Mammoth to Tower

Best Time: Mornings and Evenings

The road from Mammoth to Tower can be hit and miss with animal sightings. While the commonly seen animals in this region are Bison, Deer and Elk, the more rare sightings are what makes this a great drive. You have two options for this drive if you are heading east. You can stay on the main road or you can take the Blacktail Plateau Drive, a dirt road that is commonly known for seeing moose. To best make this choice, ask a ranger when entering the park which has had more animal sightings. Bears can be seen in this section, but ally in the spring and fall. At the date of publication, this section of road was quite active with wolf sightings. Keep an eye out for full parking lots with people on the ridges with spotting scopes.

Tower to Silvergate

Best Time: Mornings and Evenings

The road from Tower to Silvergate is one of the two most amazing wildlife viewing areas of Yellowstone National Park. Best known for the open Lamar Valley, nearly every animal in the Yellowstone can be seen here. Common sightings are bison, antelope, and coyotes, but those are not what people come out this way to see. Depending on your luck, Lamar Valley could have a "kill" visible from the road. Kills are, obviously, animals that either have died or have been killed by the region's predators. If you are near a kill, you may have an opportunity to see grizzly bears and wolves, sometimes together, feeding on the remains of an elk or bison. Bison Jams are also common along the road, so remember to be patient and enjoy the rarity of traffic jams caused by animal herds.

Tower to Canyon

Best Time: Mornings and Evenings

The road from Tower to Canyon is steep, offering some incredible views and great wildlife opportunities. While there may not be more than a few animals to see on this section of the road, those animals are bighorn sheep and bears. Bear jams are frequent along this road, with both grizzly and black bears being known to walk along the side of the road. Bighorn Sheep and grizzly bears can be seen more frequently on Chittenden Road, a dirt road leading to the Mount Washburn Trailhead. As you descend the mountain toward Canyon, watch for elk and deer.

Canyon to Norris

Best Time: Mornings and Evenings

The road from Canyon to Norris is one of three sections of the ark where animal sightings are less frequent and not as impressive as the other areas in the park. While an occasional elk, bison or even a bear can be seen along this road, chances are you will see no real signs of life. The Virginia Cascade Drive (which heads east only) is a nice road to look for animals, but keep your expectations low in this section. Keep looking, though, because moose, bear, elk and bison have been seen.

Canyon to Fishing Bridge

Best Time: Mornings and Evenings

The Road from Canyon to Fishing Bridge is the southern rival to Lamar Valley. With otter, swans, bison herds, bear and the occasional wolf sighting, hours can be spent driving back and forth along this stretch of road. While bison are common, this section lets you see them swim across rivers and walk across the road as a herd, causing incredibly long Bison Jams. While you may see others get impatient or frustrated at being held up by yet another herd of bison crossing the road, take a step away from it and think of how rare this experience is. If you see a group of people on ridges in the early morning or evening in Lamar, stop your car and ask what they see. Wolves have been known to frequent the area.

Fishing Bridge to East Entrance

Best Time: Mornings and Evenings

The road from Fishing Bridge to the East Entrance of Yellowstone is an incredibly interesting drive for a number of reasons. Not only is it more common to see bears in this region during the fall, but it is also a common area to see moose and bighorn sheep. An occasional elk or bison can be seen in this region, but it is generally known for bear, moose and sheep.

Fishing Bridge to West Thumb

Best Time: Sunrise and Sunset

The road from Fishing Bridge to West Thumb is best seen in the fall, as the elk are in the rut. With huge racks on their heads, bull elk can frequently be heard and seen bugling. While most active in the evenings and mornings, elk and bison can be seen here throughout the day. Be warned that during the summer, this section of the drive will have very few animal sightings.

West Thumb to South Entrance

The road from West Thumb to the South Entrance is a pretty drive through the woods with very few animal sightings. While bear, bison and elk are seen here, they aren't spotted frequently enough to recommend taking this drive to look for wildlife. While it may not happen, be on the lookout for animals, as they can be found anywhere in this huge park.

West Thumb to Old Faithful

West Thumb to Old Faithful is another region where there aren't a lot of animals, compared to the more active areas in the park. A few elk and bison can be seen, as can a random bear or two, but really this drive is uneventful compared to the other stretches of pavement. As with any stretch of road, an animal not normally seen in a region may be visible, so keep your eyes open for wildlife.

Madison to Old Faithful

The road from Madison to Old Faithful is best known for amazing hydrothermal activities, but it is also a great place to see bison and coyotes. While not as packed with animals as Lamar or Hayden Valley, watching wildlife along this stretch of road is like taking a trip back in time. Keep a sharp eye for hawks and foxes, as well as the rare bear sighting.

Madison to West Entrance

The road from Madison to the West Entrance is best known for elk, especially during the fall months. Once the chill returns to the air, driving this route gives amazing displays of elk in the rut. With males clashing with their huge antlers and bugling for a lucky lady, this road is occasionally like a nature documentary. Bison are also commonly seen, but not in the numbers that Lamar and Hayden Valley offer.

Madison to Norris

The road from Madison to Norris is another road that is hit or miss. Occasionally, a wolf or bear will have a kill and the area will be a hotbed of animal activity, but the majority of the year you will see bison and elk, the common theme of Yellowstone. You may see an occasional bear, but for the most part, this is a pretty drive with few animals.

SPOTTING SCOPE WATCHING

Looking for animals out of a spotting scope or through binoculars is not for everyone. While you might technically see more animals driving around the park all day, setting up a spotting scope on a ridge for the morning or evening offers quite rewarding views. If you are interested in seeing wolves, this is probably going to be how you see them.

Wolves are not creatures of habit like the other mammals of Yellowstone National Park, which makes the likelihood of seeing them from the road incredibly rare. While driving around the park, keep an eye out for ridges with numerous people standing around spotting scopes. Chances are, if there are people there, they are watching either a bear or a wolf, or waiting for one to return.

If you do watch for wildlife through binoculars or a spotting scope, anticipate spending a few hours immediately after the sun rises on a ridge, as well as two hours or so before the sunsets. Watching animals with others through spotting scopes is also a fantastic way to get updated on animal sightings, as the people who typically engage in this behavior have their own, fresh experiences.

Spotting Scope Rules

- Ask before looking through someone's scope

- Do not adjust someone's scope unless they tell you it is ok

- If you can, bring a pair of binoculars or a spotting scope and tripod, as well as snacks, a drink and extra clothing. If you want, bring up a small camp chair.

- Do not set up your scope in front of someone else's.

- Parking in popular spotting scope areas can be limited. Plan to get to the location early to guarantee not only a parking spot, but also a prime spot to set up.

WARNING: *Be aware not everyone who uses spotting scopes in the park is friendly, especially those who are looking for wolves and consider themselves to be experts. Some people will knowingly giving you false information, as they feel that the wolves need to be left alone, and only they can watch them. This warning is based on widespread reports of certain groups' behavior when it comes to wolves. The best bet is, if you see a large group of people with spotting scopes, they are watching for something cool, so ignore their rudeness and get watching for wildlife!*

HIKING AND WILDLIFE WATCHING

Hiking in nature can be scary, especially when coming across wildlife. While rare, animal attacks have occurred in nearly every National Park in America. Yellowstone is no different, as it is home to some serious animals.

Before hiking in Yellowstone, please make sure you review all information available. If you follow the rules, wildlife watching directly out in Yellowstone can be the best experience.

While we could tell you how to behave, we will instead take a direct quote from Yellowstone National Park regarding wildlife viewing:

"Wild animals, especially females with young, are unpredictable and dangerous. Keep a safe distance from all wildlife. Each year a number of park visitors are injured by wildlife when approaching too closely. Approaching on foot within 100 yards (91 m) of bears or wolves or within 25 yards (23 m) of other wildlife is prohibited. Please use roadside pullouts when viewing wildlife. Use binoculars or telephoto lenses for safe viewing and to avoid disturbing them. By being sensitive to its needs, you will see more of an animal's natural behavior and activity. If you cause an animal to move, you are too close! It is illegal to willfully remain near or approach wildlife, including birds, within ANY distance that disturbs or displaces the animal.

THE MAJOR MAMMALS OF YELLOWSTONE

There are numerous species of wildlife throughout Yellowstone National Park, but for the sake of brevity and excitement, we will focus on the animals which are the main draw for visitors.

The following pages will help you identify animals when you see them, as well as give you something to look at while you are driving around the park.

AMERICAN
BISON

No, this is not a buffalo, this is a bison. Make sure you call it by the correct name. Found throughout the park, the larger herds of bison can be found in Lamar and Hayden Valley at any hour of the day.

BLACK BEARS

Black bears are commonly found in the higher elevation areas and toward the East Entrance. They can be differentiated from grizzly bears by their size, snout and lack of a hump, as well as their color. While some black bears and be quite large, seeing one next to a grizzly erases any doubt as to which is which.

GRIZZLY BEARS

Commonly seen in Lamar and Hayden Valley, the area around Mount Washburn also has frequent sightings. These are huge bears and have a visible hump on their backs near their shoulders.

BIGHORN SHEEP

These sheep can most commonly be seen between Gardiner and Mammoth, near the bridge crossing the Lamar River and toward the East Entrance. In the early fall, watch for battling males banging their heads together at a full run.

COYOTES

Commonly mistaken for wolves, especially in Lamar and Hayden Valley, coyotes have become less frequent since the reintroduction of wolves. Smaller, skinnier, with a bushier tail, a narrower face and pointy ears, coyotes can be heard all over the park each night. Chances are, if it is mid-day and you see something that looks like a dog and is all alone, it is a coyote and not a wolf.

ELK

Elk are not as common as they used to be, thanks to wolves, but they are still pretty easy to find in the park. Larger than deer and far more majestic, the elk are best seen during the Spring and Fall months.

MOOSE

Since the 1988 fire, the majority of moose have stopped residing along the busier sections of the park, flocking to the solitude of the lake region of the park. While hard to see, they are common most common along the southern and eastern sections of the park, and are most active in the morning and evening.

MOUNTAIN GOAT

Mountain goats are not as common as one would believe, but if you really want to see one, head out to the Soda Butte Campground and scan the huge rock cliffs with a good pair of binoculars. These cliff dwellers are tough to see, but are impressively agile on the rockiest of terrains

DEER

Yellowstone has two types of deer that are common to see: the Mule Deer and White-Tailed Deer. Mule Deer, named after their huge, mule like ears are the most common deer in Yellowstone. They can be found all over the park. White-Tailed Deer are less common and are named for their white tail.

GRAY WOLVES

Seeing a Gray Wolf is an incredible experience and one I hope you get to have on your trip to Yellowstone. These huge canines are most often seen from a distance, and even then for just a few minutes. While there are wolf packs across the park, the most common sightings occur in the Lamar and Hayden Valley and more recently along the road between Mammoth and Canyon. For detailed pack information, please stop by the Yellowstone Institute stores, where they sell a pamphlet that tells about the wolf packs and their locations.

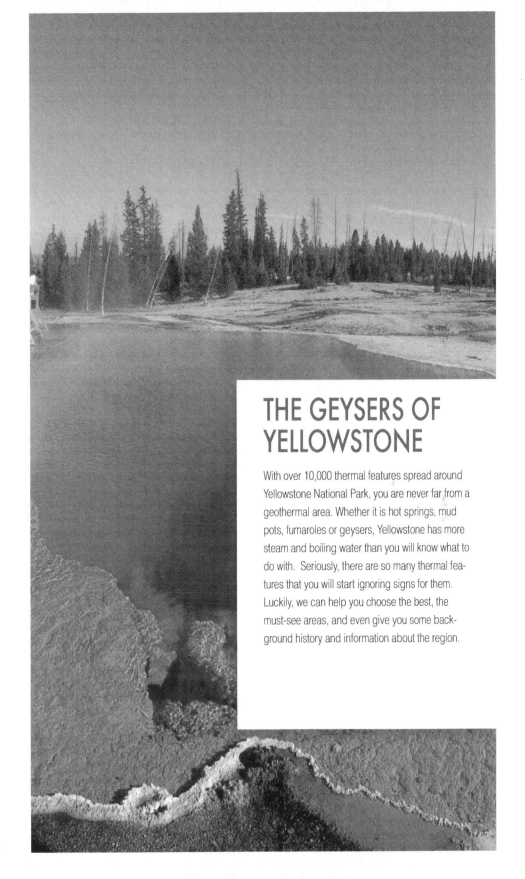

THE GEYSERS OF YELLOWSTONE

With over 10,000 thermal features spread around
Yellowstone National Park, you are never far from a
geothermal area. Whether it is hot springs, mud
pots, fumaroles or geysers, Yellowstone has more
steam and boiling water than you will know what to
do with. Seriously, there are so many thermal features that you will start ignoring signs for them.
Luckily, we can help you choose the best, the
must-see areas, and even give you some background history and information about the region.

Yellowstone is home to 60% of the world's geysers. There are five different types of thermal features in Yellowstone, each different and unique, but it is best to think of them as part of one greater region. Most of the geothermal areas in Yellowstone National Park sit inside the caldera of the super-volcano that is Yellowstone, with molten rock as little as two and a half miles below your feet. As the "liquid hot magma" heats the groundwater, the gas and boiling water, must escape somewhere. Releasing pressure is the extremely basic reason why there are so many geysers and thermal features around Yellowstone.

Fumaroles

Plain and simple, fumaroles blast steam and gas, but not water. They are vents in the ground that often hiss and expel steam from their holes. The fumaroles can expel carbon dioxide and sulfur dioxide. In Yellowstone, the estimated 4,000 fumaroles can be best seen at the Black Growler Steam Vent at the Norris Geyser Basin

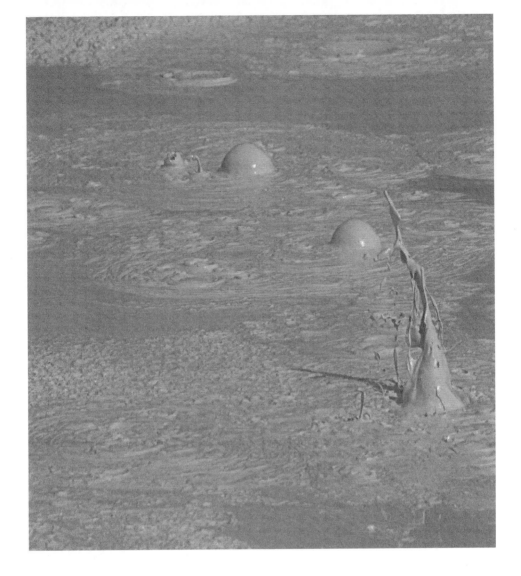

Mud Pots

Mud Pots are a personal favorite, especially after a heavy rain. While the other thermal features may offer clear pools of boiling hot water, or boiling water being shot up into the heavens, mud pots are more laid back. They aren't beautiful or colorful, but they are something you won't see anywhere else. Mud pots are small pools of mud that slowly boil. While some mud pots are less mud and more water, the best mud pots look like slowly boiling clay, expanding in bubbles and breaking in chunks of flying hot mud. The best mud pots can be seen at Artist Paint Pots and Fountain Paint Pots.

Hot Springs

Hot Springs are the second biggest draw to the park, geothermally speaking. While some are small, some of the largest hot springs in the world at in Yellowstone. Colorful, from bacteria that make the hot springs home, these often deep pools give you a chance to peer into the center of the earth! The best area is near the grand Prismatic Hot Spring. While walking by hot springs, be aware that the temperature difference from the steam to the normal air can be quite shocking, even on a hot summer day.

Geysers

Geysers are the number one geothermal draw to the park, the most famous of which is Old Faithful. Geysers come in two shapes, either fountain geysers or cone geysers. Fountain geysers appear to have a much more violent eruption, as they typically come from what appears to be a regular hot spring. Cone geysers are the more beautiful of the geysers, shooting boiling water and steam out of a small hole at the top of a cone. Many of these are visible, but dormant in the park.

Travertine Terraces

The terraces are most commonly seen at Mammoth, where pools of water gather above and slowly drain down the hillside. Over time, the limestone, which the hot springs sit on, breaks down and small amounts of travertine and calcium carbonate are brought to the surface through the thermal waters. The chalky white substance is deposited along the terraces, forming the leveled terraces Mammoth is most famous for.

THE SEVEN ROADSIDE
GEYSER AREAS OF
YELLOWSTONE

Norris Geyser Basin

Why: Norris Geyser Basin in home to the world's tallest active geyser, as well as some of the most colorful hot springs you will ever see. Vivid colors, the stench of sulfur (which smells like rotten egg), and steam rising from the ground as far as you can see make Norris a fantastic place to fall in love with the geysers of Yellowstone. With 2.25 miles of trails, exploring Norris is a great way to spend a few hours in the afternoon.

Best Time: Any

Best Features: Steamboat Geyser, but it can easily be years between eruptions. It is the world's tallest active geyser and its eruptions can shoot more than 300 feet into to the air anywhere from three to 40 minutes at a time.

Smell Factor: Strong

Upper Geyser Basin

Why: Home to Old Faithful, as well as the largest number of features in the park, the 150 hydrothermal features of this Geyser Basin are some of the most famous in the world. Five major geysers can be predicted here, and your chances of seeing a huge geyser erupt are pretty good, as long as you are patient. With fantastic boardwalks and views of the entire basin, spending a few hours here is not just a good idea, but is required to experience the park.

Best Time: Sunrise or sunset to avoid the crowds

Best Features: Castle, Grand, Daisy, and Riverside Geysers, as well as Old Faithful

Smell Factor: Minimal

Midway Geyser Area

Why: While Midway may not seem like much from the road, this geyser basin located next to the Firehole River is nearly as important to see as Old Faithful. While there are numerous pretty sights at Midway, including watching hot water get dumped into the much cooler Firehole River, there are two main attractions. First is Excelsior Geyser, which is a huge crater (200 by300 feet) that pumps over 4,000 gallons of water each minute into the river. While that is rad, it isn't as impressive as the size and colors of Grand Prismatic Spring. Grand Prismatic isn't just the largest hot spring in Yellowstone; it is also one of the most photographed hot springs in the world. At 370 feet in diameter and over 121 feet deep, the mind has a difficult time comprehending the awesomeness that this place is.

Best Time: Sunset

Best Features: Grand Prismatic Hot Spring

Smell Factor: Minimal

Lower Geyser Basin

Why: The Lower Geyser Basin is home to a few awesome features that every Yellowstone visitor needs to see. Starting with the Fountain Paint Pots, this region is smelly and wonderful. At only half a mile long, the boardwalk loop of Lower Geyser Basin makes for a great stroll. While the main draw is the Fountain Paint Pots, the entire loop offers pretty rad geyser experiences.

If walking along a boardwalk isn't your thing, the Lower Geyser Basin area offers a great three mile drive called Firehole Lake Drive. This one-way road has numerous thermal features, but the main draw is the Great Fountain, which erupts twice daily. Sadly, the geyser isn't as predictable as Old Faithful, so waiting here may be required. Signs are posted at the Geyser for predicted eruptions, but they have a two hour window when it could erupt.

Best Time: Afternoon and evening

Best Features: Fountain Paint Pots, Great Fountain, Spasm Geyser

Smell Factor: Moderate

West Thumb Geyser Basin

Why: This is the largest geyser basin overlooking Yellowstone Lake and is the same size as the caldera region of Crater Lake, Oregon. While this is one of the smallest geyser areas in the park, it does consist of nearly every type of thermal feature that Yellowstone has to offer. With mud pots, hot springs, deep pools, fumaroles and even lake shore geysers, stopping here gives an insight to what the bottom of Yellowstone Lake is like. The West Thumb area has been seeing a decrease in thermal activity, but if you are in the area, seeing a boiling pool right under the surface of the lake is a pretty cool experience. Also, gazing in the Abyss Pool is a great place to watch the awesome colors of the pool contrast against the blues of the sky and whites of the clouds.

Best Time: Sunrise and Sunsets in the Fall

Best Features: Abyss Pool, Fishing Cone

Smell Factor: Minimal

Mammoth Hot Springs Area

Why: While Mammoth isn't as grand as it used to be, walking the Terrace is a rite of passage for all Yellowstone visitors. Since the late 1800s, visitors have stood in awe at the mysterious pools and terrace features at Mammoth. While the water level has been low in recent years, the region goes through cycles of awesomeness. The next good spring and summer should be 2015 and 2016, but that doesn't mean you should skip it during other years. While a drive to the upper Terrace can be done, take some time if you can and walk from the Mammoth Visitor area, up the terrace boardwalk and around the loop. Doing this helps you appreciate the size and scale of the area in a way that driving does not.

Mammoth is not for everyone, but as we said, it should be experienced by all. While many visitors will be jaded by the lack of activity in the region, take some time, sit back and fully appreciate the rarity and uniqueness of the Mammoth Terrace. Nowhere else will you see such a display, so enjoy it!

Best Time: Cool Mornings

Best Features: Minerva Spring and Terrace, Canary Spring and Terrace, Liberty Cap

Smell Factor: Minimal

Mud Volcano Geyser Area

Why: Discovered in the 1870s by the Washburn Expedition, visitors today will feel the same sense of awe and wonder that the explorers did back in the day. On quiet mornings, the Mud Volcano area can be heard from quite a distance away, booming and sloshing across the otherwise quiet southern end of Hayden Valley. In the 1870s, the region could be heard from miles away. While the sounds of the region may have quieted down some, the activity is still as amazing as ever. Strong smelling sulfur lurks around every corner and the walk around the geyser is a journey for all of your senses. With epic sounding features such as Black Dragon's Caldron, Sour Lake, and Mud Caldron Sulfur Caldron, this is a favorite for visitors of all ages.

Best Time: Any

Best Features: Dragons Mouth, Black Dragon's Caldron and the Mud Volcano.

Smell Factor: Strong

6 SIMPLE, YET IMPORTANT RULES FOR GEYSER BASINS

We should assume that each and every visitor to thermal features will understand that they are hot, dangerous and deadly. However, each and every year tourists get injured and/or die because they don't follow the signs along the routes. Thermal features are dangerous, often hot enough to kill you instantly or over painful, agonizing days of blistering and skin peeling.

Follow All Signs

If you step off the boardwalks, you could die. The crust between the thermal features is thin and can break at any time. Even if you see an elk or bison walking on an area, be aware that numerous animals fall through and die each year.

Do Not Test How Warm the Water is

As tempting as it is to lean down and touch the water, don't do it. It doesn't feel any different than normal water, really. If you want to feel hot water, go home, boil water and put your hand in it; you will accomplish the same thing.

Do Not Touch the Bacteria Mats

Again, this should be common knowledge, but numerous tourists have tried to carve their initials in the numerous bacteria mats around the park. Not only does it look ugly, but it is also destroying years, decades or centuries of nature's work in a matter of seconds. Let everyone enjoy it and don't touch. The oils from your hands can forever ruin an area with just one touch.

Hold On to Your Belongings and Garbage

The geyser basins can be quite windy and are littered with hats, sunglasses, scarfs and garbage from careless tourists. Hold on to your stuff and refrain from littering.

Do Not Toss Anything In to Thermal Features

Numerous thermal features have been destroyed by careless, irresponsible, idiot tourists who have thought it would be cool/fun to throw change, sticks, garbage or any other object into them. These features are delicate, and while sticks and other natural objects may fall into them, it isn't your job to replicate a natural event.

Do Not Take Your Dog On the Boardwalk

National Park rules prohibit pets from any hike or trail. It doesn't matter if your dog is the best-behaved dog in the world and would never leave your side, they are not allowed. They should be kept inside your vehicle at all times, unless you are at a designated dog-friendly area. To prevent them from running off, causing harm to others or themselves, keep them on a leash. Why so harsh with animals in the park, you ask?

Let me tell you a true story:

WARNING: GRAPHIC STORY

In July of 1981, a man was driving through Yellowstone and decided to stop at the Fountain Paint Pot area of the Lower Geyser Basin. He was traveling with his friend and his dog and when they arrived to the parking lot, the dog escaped and ran down the boardwalk. As it sprinted down past scores of tourists, it noticed the Celestine Pool, which has a temperature of over 200 degrees Fahrenheit. Without hesitation, it jumped into the pool and immediately started yelping. The man, who was running after his dog, decided to jump headfirst into the spring to save his dog. The heat immediately got to him and he struggled back to the boardwalk, unable to save the dog. As the dog boiled and died before the now gathering crowds, the man lay on the boardwalk, exclaiming to his friend that his actions were stupid.

As the man lay there waiting for help, his skin immediately started peeling and cracking, and when a bystander tried to remove his steaming shoes from his feet, his skin, muscles and tendons came off with his shoes and socks, like per

Throwing coins, rocks or other objects into pools is illegal.

You can be fined up to $5,000 for throwing objects into a hot spring or geyser.

Why is it illegal to throw things into hot springs?

- Coins and other objects become coated with silica and can plug and destroy geysers and hot springs. Once destroyed,

fectly cooked chicken off the bone. He sustained third degree burns over his entire body and died after 16 hours of agonizing pain.

The dog's body was removed from the pool as best as park officials could, but the oils from its rotting corpse were visible in the water for years.

While this should be an isolated instance, there are numerous stories of people getting severely burned and/or dying from touching, jumping in or breaking through the crust to fall into the the thermal features of Yellowstone. **Be smart, be safe and follow all rules and regulations.**

HIKING IN YELLOWSTONE

Yellowstone National Park features hundreds of hikes, though the average visitor doesn't leave a half-mile radius of their car or camp. While some of this can be attributed to the layout of Yellowstone, with roads next to most of the major scenic areas, the reality of this statistic is sheer laziness by most American tourists to the region. There is no excuse to not explore the trails of Yellowstone National Park.With so many trailheads spread throughout the park, it is difficult to decide which

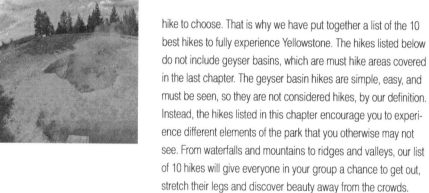

hike to choose. That is why we have put together a list of the 10 best hikes to fully experience Yellowstone. The hikes listed below do not include geyser basins, which are must hike areas covered in the last chapter. The geyser basin hikes are simple, easy, and must be seen, so they are not considered hikes, by our definition. Instead, the hikes listed in this chapter encourage you to experience different elements of the park that you otherwise may not see. From waterfalls and mountains to ridges and valleys, our list of 10 hikes will give everyone in your group a chance to get out, stretch their legs and discover beauty away from the crowds.

5 TIPS FOR HIKING IN YELLOWSTONE

Carry the Ten Essentials

We get that carrying the 10 Essentials on every single hike, no matter the length or difficulty level sounds a bit insane, but we want to reassure you it isn't. While you might never need a map and a compass, having a kit with all of the 10 essentials in a pack is a great habit to get into. If for no other reason, carry everything on the list to always have snacks, sunscreen and water.

The Ten Essentials

1) Map

2) Compass/GPS

3) Extra Food

4) Extra Water

5) Extra Clothes

6) Headlamp/Flashlight

7) A First Aid Kit

8) Sunglasses and Sunscreen

9) Fire Starter

10) Knife

Be Bear Aware

Yellowstone is bear country, and while it might be nice to think that the worst a bear can do is steal your pic-a-nic basket, the reality is that bears can be aggressive and deadly. While hiking, talk loudly and keep your eyes and ears open for any noise you don't recognize. While bear encounters are pretty rare while hiking, it is best to remember to give animals their distance. The majority of bear attacks in Yellowstone come from sows protecting their cubs, so if you see a mother and cub or just a cub, walk far away from the area, loudly. Do not, and I repeat, do not go back to your car to grab your camera and return to take pictures. A man did this in 2013 and was attacked by the mother bear.

Ask Rangers about Animal Activity in the Area

The best way to stay safe on the trails of Yellowstone is to ask a ranger about the current trail conditions and inquire about possible animal activity. They will be honest and straightforward about whether you should hike the trail you are asking about and may even suggest better, safer alternatives. The NPS rangers are some of the best resources for information, so if you see one, take the time to say hello, thank them for keeping the park safe and ask them where you can find all the great animal trails. If they can't help you, they can direct you to someone who can.

Stay on Trails

What may seem like the simplest of rules could be the one that saves your life. In most places of the world, stepping off the trail doesn't typically risk your life. In Yellowstone, many of the hikes you may take are along geyser basins. Geyser basins may appear strong and you will probably see a bison walking along an area closed to humans, but don't let that convince you that stepping off trail is a smart idea. Numerous bison die each year after falling through the thin crust over geysers and hot springs.

Take Only Pictures, Leave Only Footprints

We are lucky enough to have a country that sets aside our most beautiful lands from development, supposedly being protected forever. The National Parks are nature in some of its purest forms, so don't ruin it by leaving garbage everywhere. Pick up all trash, including banana peels, orange peels, apple cores and any other non-native object that you see. We want the parks to be around for our grandchildren's grandchildren, so be a conscientious steward of the land and respect nature in all ways, shapes and forms.

THE 10 BEST DAY HIKES IN
YELLOWSTONE

Uncle Tom's Trail

Distance: .6 Miles Round Trip

Elevation Gain: 500 Feet

Difficulty: Moderate (May cause vertigo)

Location: Canyon

Why: Originally constructed in 1898, this terrifying trail is sure to get any waterfall lover excited about life. Dropping down from the Canyon Rim toward the Lower Yellowstone Falls, this trail offers a gorgeous and unique view of one of the most photographed waterfalls in America. While some consider this a trail, it is really a few hundred steps down a staircase, with see-through steps along an exposed canyon. The views are worth the trek, and after you see how the first visitors travelled down the cliff, you will be glad you are alive today and not in the early 1900s.

The trail is named "Uncle' Tom's Trail" because the original route to the base of the falls was created and operated by H. F. Henderson, who had the nickname, Uncle Tom. He would charge visitors $1 to explore the base of the falls. While successful for a few years, the new roads and trails built by the National Park Service directly impacted him. As a result Uncle Tom's business began to decline. By 1907, he was out of business, but the National Park has continued to maintain the trail and named it after him.

Wraith Falls

Distance: .8 Miles Round Trip

Elevation Gain: 100 Feet

Difficulty: Easy

Location: East of Mammoth

Why: Wraith Falls is one of the easiest and more fun waterfall hikes in Yellowstone. While it is a popular hike, it has nowhere near the crowds of the roadside waterfalls. It is a short and mostly flat trail, this path is less of a hike and more of a leisurely stroll alongside raspberries, over a wooden footbridge to a waterfall that cascades down a rocky outcropping in a small forest of Douglas Fir trees. Tumbling down 100 feet, Wraith Falls is always scenic and a great little hike for a picnic lunch on.

The last section of the trail is the steepest park of the hike, gaining 50 feet of elevation in just one tenth of a mile. For most hikers, this is nothing, but if you bringing small children on this hike, this is probably where they will start getting whiney. Bring a snack, head up the switchbacks, and get ready for an awesome view!

Artist Paint Pots

Distance: 1.2 Miles Round Trip

Elevation Gain: 100 feet

Difficulty: Easy for most

Location: Between Norris and Madison

Why: If you love the geyser basins around the park, but are looking for something a little less crowded with far fewer boardwalks, this is the perfect trail for you. At just over a mile long, weaving through the forests of the Gibbon meadows, the very wide and flat trail is a perfect location for a family stroll into the wilderness of Yellowstone. The Artist Paint Pots themselves are not as impressive as the other geyser basins, but on the right morning they can emit large amounts of steam, impressive bubbles of mud and the soothing stench of sulfur.

The Artist Paint Pots are actually a favorite for photographers of all abilities, as the layout seems much more natural than the other basin trails. With just a few visible man-made objects, this thermal feature location gives great insight on how it was to travel in the park before the days of millions of yearly tourists.

Mystic Falls

Distance: 3 Mile Loop

Elevation Gain: 300 Feet

Difficulty: Moderate

Location: North of Old Faithful

Why: Mystic Falls is another waterfall that needs to be seen. It is a true representative of rocky mountain waterfalls; a small cascade tumbling down 70 feet between sparse trees, but with a Yellowstone twist. Steam from thermal activity can be spotted along the entire length of the waterfall. While this trail is best seen in the spring and in the early mornings, it is a great hike whenever you have the chance.

Mystic Falls, originally named Firehole Falls, is considered by many to be the best short waterfall trail in Yellowstone. What makes the trail a great hike isn't just the waterfall with steam vents (though that is pretty rad), it is the combination of the falls and the view of the Upper Geyser Basin from the ridge. If you have ever wanted to see the thermal features of Old Faithful from a distance, this short loop trail is exactly what you need.

Fairy Falls

Distance: 5 Miles Round Trip

Elevation Gain: Minimal

Difficulty: Easy

Location: North of Old Faithful

Why: This easy to follow, well-maintained trail can get quite busy, but resting your eyes on a 200-foot high waterfall against a rocky cave makes you forget about that. Fairy Falls is one of the best waterfalls in Yellowstone, and you get to hike along a trail to the base of it. The waterfall itself can look quite sparse, but that is mainly due to the immensity of the cliff at which you are watching it tumble down. With two thirds of the waterfall coming down dark rock that Is carved out from erosion, the scale of the waterfall become apparent.

Fairy Falls can be a crowded trail, with little shade. Do not let the lack of parking or the stifling heat stop you from walking this trail. The first time I hiked this trail, I rounded a corner and came almost face to face with a moose. The trail is amazing, full of possibilities and rewards you with a fantastic waterfall.

Elephant Back Mountain Trail

Distance: 2.8 Miles Round Trip

Elevation Gain: 800 feet

Difficulty: Moderate

Location: Between Bridge Bay and West Thumb

Why: If you have wondered where one of the best views of Yellowstone Lake is, this is the answer to your question. Climbing just under 1,000 feet, the trail to Elephant Back Mountain is immaculate and not as steep as one might think. With older trees along this hike, the forests are more spread open, allowing you to look around and possibly spot a pine marten.

The best time to hike this is just before sunrise, as the east facing view will let you watch the morning light shine through the mountains to the east and across the lake. The view here is extremely rewarding, and taking the time to hike here can lift your trip out of the "good" and into the "great" category.

Grand Canyon of Yellowstone Trails

Distance: Varies

Elevation Gain: Varies

Difficulty: Easy to Moderate

Location: Canyon

Why: One of the two most-famous, gorgeous, and awe-inspiring waterfalls in Yellowstone, the upper and lower falls along the Grand Canyon of Yellowstone make for great hiking and sightseeing. Tower Falls to the north is pretty and needs to be seen, but the Grand Canyon of Yellowstone makes the scenery of the entire park even more impressive.

Numerous trails extend from the canyon and offer fantastic views of the waterfall, the canyon and the pristine forests surrounding the region. For the best hiking advice and animal updates, check in with the rangers at the Canyon Visitor Center.

Mount Washburn

Distance: 6.4 Miles Round Trip

Elevation Gain: 1,400 feet

Difficulty: Moderate

Location: Between Canyon and Tower Falls

Why: I consider this a must hike trail. As one of the tallest points in the park, this trail is a trek up a mountain to a fire lookout station with views of nearly the entire span of Yellowstone National Park. With frequent Bighorn Sheep sightings, occasionally grizzly sightings and a chance to tour around inside the lookout, passing on this hike is not allowed. This trail is consistently described as one of the best day hikes in Yellowstone, and I agree whole-heartedly. From ridiculously perfect views of the Grand Canyon of Yellowstone to a panoramic view that will leave you speechless, hiking here is a thing of beauty.

Get here early in the morning, to ensure you have a place to park. Also, while hiking expect to see a few hikers calling it quits before the summit, as the elevation can fatigue less-experienced hikers. Make sure you also plan for all weather possibilities, as wind, rain, thunderstorms or snow can appear without much warning.

Pebble Creek

Distance: 10.8 Miles Round Trip

Elevation Gain: 1,000 feet

Difficulty: Moderate to Advanced

Location: Near Cooke City and the Northeast Entrance

Why: In order to fully comprehend just how rugged the area surrounding Yellowstone is, it is best to trek up into the hills, and that is exactly what the Pebble Creek Trail does. Gaining the majority of elevation in the first mile, the trail gives amazing views of the areas rugged mountains. Hiking through a high valley, animals are often seen, but the highlight is always the views. High alpine valleys, specifically in this region of the country are amazing sights and are not to be passed up.

Keep in mind that this is a real trail with little signage and used far less than any trail we have previously mentioned. A ford of Pebble Creek is more often than not needed, so bring proper footwear with you. Knowledge of hiking is a requirement for this trail, as there are numerous forks and campsites along the trail. That being said, if you have hiked a bit, you should have no problem with this trail. Enjoy the views

Specimen Ridge

Distance: 17.7

Elevation Gain: 4142 Feet

Difficulty: Moderate to Advanced

Location: Between Tower and Cooke City

Why: If every other hike here has left you unimpressed, the Specimen Ridge Trail above the grass-lands of the Lamar Valley will bring you joy. This 17.7 mile trek is a shuttle hike, meaning that the trailhead and the end of the trail (along the same road) are quite a distance apart and you will need to hitch a ride back to the first trailhead. Do not worry about finding a ride; this is a well-used section of the park. The trail offers a summit of Amethyst Mountain for you peak baggers, as well as some of the most amazing panoramic views the park has to offer.

Sure, you will have to ford the Lamar River after 15.6 miles of hiking, but that is what makes this trail great.

If wildlife watching is your thing, this trail takes you above some of the most active regions for wild-life in the park. Frequently, hikers along this trail have reported numerous sightings of bear, wolves, moose, elk, bison and antelope. While there are very few examples of thermal activity along this trail, this area is the perfect representation of the wilderness of Yellowstone. Hike this trail if you want to see bison fighting, ford a swift river and hike for hours on end with little shade. If that sounds interesting to you (it should!), do not pass on this trail!

MORE HIKE NAMES TO KEEP IN MIND

Observation Point: 1.1 Miles in the Old Faithful Area

Trout Lake Trail: 1 Mile near the Northeast Entrance

Lake Overlook Trail: 2 Miles near West Thumb

Bunsen Peak Trail: 4 Miles near Golden Gate

Purple Mountain Trail: 6 Miles near Madison Campground

Tower Falls: .2 Miles near Tower

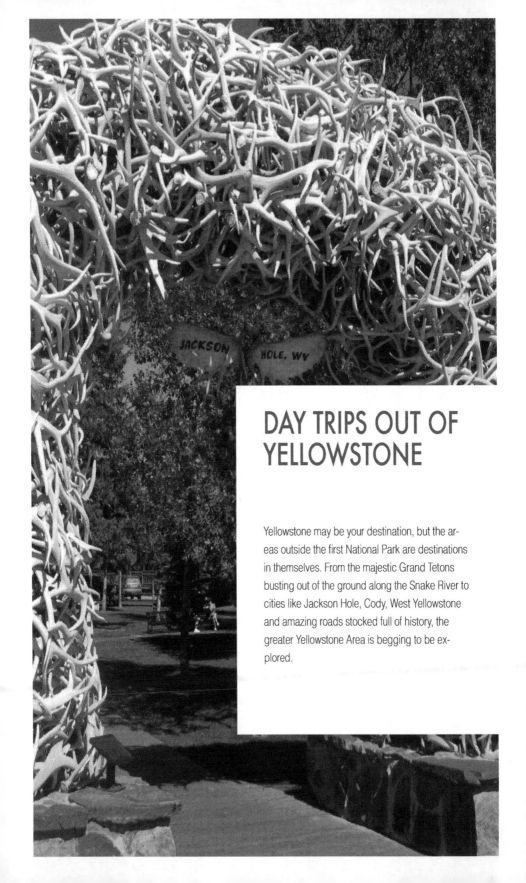

DAY TRIPS OUT OF YELLOWSTONE

Yellowstone may be your destination, but the areas outside the first National Park are destinations in themselves. From the majestic Grand Tetons busting out of the ground along the Snake River to cities like Jackson Hole, Cody, West Yellowstone and amazing roads stocked full of history, the greater Yellowstone Area is begging to be explored.

Exploring the regions outside the park will give you better insight into culture, fashion and history of the region.

Starting in the Grand Tetons and working our way around the park in a counter clockwise manner, we will give you the best activities to do in each city, along each road and in each area. With spectacular views, one of the best museums in the West and a trip along Chief Joseph's route where he and his people tried to escape the Calvary, day trips outside out Yellowstone are full of incredibly rare pieces of American history.

Take some time, peruse the following pages and find a day trip that will help your vacation become the stuff of legends.

GRAND TETON NATIONAL PARK

The Five Can't Miss Spots of Grand Teton National Park

While you could spend days, weeks, or even months exploring all there is to see around the Tetons, most road trips have a time schedule and a budget. That is why we took the time to highlight the five best activities and areas of the region.

From famous pull off spots that have been photographed by Ansel Adams to a classic hike that gives you a chance to explore the rugged mountains, taking a day trip to the Grand Tetons and stopping at our five recommended sites will give you a great taste for the Tetons. If you choose one or all five, you will get a great experience in this gorgeous, underrated National Park just south of Yellowstone.

Jenny Lake

Jenny Lake may be the greatest little lake in the Tetons. With kayak, canoe and boat rentals, as well as a ferry service to one of the best hikes in the region, exploring Jenny Lake is a great place to spend a few hours and discover the beauty of the Tetons. With a great visitor center, plenty of parking and a chance to get away from the crowds to take in the view, stopping at Jenny is much needed. If you only get one chance to learn about and explore the Tetons, Jenny Lake is the best place to do just that.

At Jenny Lake, seriously think about renting a boat or taking a scenic cruise. Remember you are on vacation, so try to do something awesome! Take an evening cruise during sunset, as Jenny Lake is one of the best places to see the setting sun in the world.

Snake River Overlook

If you are a fan of Ansel Adams, or have ever seen a beautiful picture of the grand Tetons and the Snake River, chances are, the
picture was taken from the Snake River Overlook. This roadside
overlook is super popular at sunrise and sunsets, so if you want
to get the perfect picture, show up early. Even if you are just passing through during midday, the view is spectacular and definitely
one of the places that you must get a picture from.

Remember though; take some time to watch the scenery unfold
before your eyes without your camera, as nature is something
you need to experience as best you can. If you happen to be in
the region any time near sunset, take the time and watch it from
here. You won't regret it!

Inspiration Point

Every guidebook says "If you can do just one hike...", and we
are no better. If you can hike only one trail in the Tetons, do NOT
waste your time with any other trail. The Inspiration Point is hike is
a fantastic day trip into the Tetons. While it does get crowded, the
views don't get much better. At six miles, including a boat ride
across Jenny Lake, the trail takes you up a gap in the massive
mountains, past a spectacular waterfall

and up a trail carved out of the rock to a view of Wyoming you
need to experience. If you want to extend it, a trek up to Cascade Canyon and Lake Solitude (15 miles round trip) gets you in
the heart of the Teton Range and away from the crowds. Trust us
when we say, this is a hike you need to travel. We basically wrote
about the Tetons just so you would come here.

Craig Thomas Discovery & Visitor Center at Moose

The other visitor centers in the Tetons are great, but if you must choose one to stop at, the Moose Visitor Center is pretty awesome. Full of educational information, as well as a cool display on the climbing history of the Teton Range, stopping here will help answer any questions you may have on the National Park. It also has Wi-Fi, but you will be too overwhelmed by the state of the art exhibits, ranger talks and a fantastic documentary to want to play with your phone.

Moose-Wilson Road

Often overlooked by the uninformed, the Moose-Wilson Road is one of the most scenic roads in the greater Jackson/Teton Region. At just eight miles long, the road weaves through hillsides and wetlands, the latter of which are best known for frequent moose sightings. The road passes next to the Laurence S. Rockefeller Preserve Center, which is a great spot for wildlife watching, as well as a fantastic moose habitat.

Early mornings and evenings are the best time to experience this road if you want to see moose, but also be aware that this eight mile road is home to both black and grizzly bears, so use caution if you get out of the car.

EXPLORING JACKSON HOLE

The city of Jackson Hole is the home to ex-Vice President and known smirker, Dick Cheney. However, it is best known for amazing skiing and snowboarding in a town that still looks like the Old West. Just south of the mountains, Jackson Hole is called a "Hole" because that it how the early trappers and mountain men described how it felt to climb down from the higher elevations to the valley.

With picturesque views from nearly every street, Jackson Hole offers shopping, museums, amazing food, fantastic bars and a town square that will forever be etched in your memory.

The City Square and Shopping

Jackson has grown in the past hundred years, yet the town square still feels like you are walking back in the old west. Raised wooden boardwalks frame the main downtown shopping region, and the town square/park with impressive archways made from elk antlers. Touristy bars, restaurants and stores surround the park, and all should be explored.

From gimmicky tourist goods and chaps and Stetsons to ice cream and one of the most awesome fur stores around, walking along the boardwalk around town will take care of your shopping needs. After the shopping, grab a beverage at one of the best restaurants and bars in the West, the Million Dollar Cowboy Bar. Prized for their western memorabilia, unique pine architecture, animal mounts and the always classy genuine saddle barstools, having a drink here is much needed for so many reasons.

The National Museum of Wildlife Art

Perched on a hillside overlooking the National Elk Refuge, this museum is beautifully designed to look like it blends into the hillside. Built of rock from around the region, the building was inspired by the ruins of Slains Castle in Scotland. Full of some of the best wildlife art you have ever seen, this museum is often overlooked. If you are a fan of good art and animals, you need to stop here for a few hours. The National Museum of Wildlife Art is one of the true hidden gems of the region. Thousands of pictures, sculptures, and exhibits from around the world give you get a glimpse of the amazing art that people create, but also lets you see animals from the region and from around the world.

National Elk Refuge

Depending on when you visit the National Elk Refuge in Jackson, your experience will vary. In the winter, elk are commonly seen in droves at the refuge, as this is a sanctuary for them during each winter migration. In the summer, the Refuge isn't too crowded with animals, but does offer some amazing views of the Tetons to the Northwest.

With few hiking trails, the refuge in the off season is nothing more than a great scenic drive with the possibility of seeing a coyote, cougar, bison or elk. To get a better feel for the refuge, take a short drive to the Jackson Hole & Greater Yellowstone Visitor Center.

River Rafting

While Jackson Hole is most commonly associated with winter activities like skiing and snowboarding, it is also an awesome spot to take a whitewater rafting trip or scenic float trip. Some whitewater rafting companies offer kayaking tours on Lake Yellowstone, so if you are a fan of activities on the water check into this.

We don't have a favorite company, but the people at Jackson Hole Whitewater do a great job and are highly rated online.

THE DRIVE FROM THE NORTHEAST ENTRANCE TO CODY, WYOMING

The drive from Cooke City, Montana to Cody, Wyoming is not only one of the prettiest roads you will ever drive, it is also a great route for history. Best known for wide views, fantastic rock formations, incredible mountains and awe-inspiring viewpoints, this drive is one of the most incredible roads in America. The Beartooth Highway and the equally impressive Chief Joseph Scenic Highway form the one of the most scenic day trips you could take. The drive is 76 miles from Cooke City to Cody. It take you nearly two hours with no stops, but be prepared for it to take three hours.

Leaving Yellowstone, you will enter Silver Gate-Cooke City, which are two small little cities with a cool summer time atmosphere. While there is not much in town, aside from a few places to stay and eat, the general feel of the town is quite interesting. What used to be a little visited old mining outpost, Cooke City now has vegan restaurants and everything else that comes with road trips. The locals are quite proud of their past, and may not be as friendly as you would prefer, but keep in mind they liked seclusion and live there for a reason. Once you leave Cooke City near the Northeast Entrance of Yellowstone you start driving the most scenic drive in America, the Beartooth Highway. At 68 miles long to Red Lodge Montana, the Beartooth Highway is the highest road in both Montana and Wyoming. At

10,350 feet and 10,947 respectively, the Beartooth Highway gives some of the most impressive panoramas seen from a paved road. While the road heads out of Yellowstone's Northeast Entrance all the way to Red Lodge, Montana, we advise you to drive the Beartooth Highway as far as the Wyoming-Montana Border. From here, turn around and head back the way you came until you reach the intersection with the Chief Joseph Scenic Highway

Sidenote: *The Beartooth Highway was built in 1936; the highway follows the route of Civil War General Philip Sheridan and 120 of his men after a trip to inspect Fort Yellowstone in 1872.*

Once you reach the intersection of the Beartooth Highway and the Chief Joseph Scenic Highway, follow the signs to Cody, Wyoming. While the Beartooth offered rugged mountains, the Chief Joseph Highway shows off amazing vistas, deep canyons, awesome plateaus and a road lined with cows and deer. The highlight for many is Sunshine Creek Bridge, which spans across an impressive 400 foot canyon. Pull-off locations near the top of the pass should be appreciated for not only their view, but for their historical significance.

Named after Chief Joseph of the Nez Perce Tribe, the highway is the route that, in 1877, Chief Joseph took his people as he attempted to flee the U.S. Cavalry and enter into Canada. Signs documenting historical significance are at most of the pull off spots, allowing you to gain an understanding of the region and connect with it on a more historical level.

BUFFALO BILL CENTER OF THE WEST IN CODY, WYOMING

Fifty miles from the East Entrance of Yellowstone National Park, the town of Cody sits quietly above a deep canyon that holds the Shoshone River. While Cody only boasts a population of around 10,000 people, the city houses some awesome activities that make the long drive out of the park worth the effort. Cody calls itself the Rodeo Capitol of the World, and the town's culture and architecture mirror that moniker.

Cody is a town of the Old West, and it still clings to that image today. If you happen to be in town on an evening between June 1st and August 31st, you could possibly take part in an amateur rodeo that occurs nightly. If you happen to be in town July 1st through the 4th, you will be able to see the Cody Stampede Rodeo, an annual event that hasn't missed a year since 1919. If rodeos aren't your thing, Cody still has its best surprise waiting for you, the Buffalo Bill Center of the West.

BUFFALO BILL CENTER OF THE WEST

Home to five museums, the Buffalo Bill Center of the West is the best collection of "the west" anywhere in the world. With one of the best research libraries for the region, as well as so many displays that you are told a proper tour takes two full days, a stop here will give even the most stubborn person in your car a day of happiness and awesome memories.

The museum was started in 1917, as a way to honor Buffalo Bill. Eventually, the museum expanded to a small log cabin and a few other designs before it became the state of the art building it is today. The museum offers numerous seasonal exhibits that are all worthy of a few hours of wandering around.

Starting with the Buffalo Bill Museum, interact with hologram Buffalo Bills while looking at his impact on showcasing the Old West to full crowds around the world. With hundreds of thousands of things to see or read the Buffalo Bill portion will give you a detailed tour of nearly every aspect of the man's life, including his childhood home, which was brought to the museum.

Initially, the Buffalo Bill Museum ignored the people he exploited the most, the Native Americans, so a new, amazing, and respectful exhibit honors them at the Plains Indians Museum. Focusing on the life, culture, traditions and values held by the Plains Indians, the collection of artifacts in this section are amazing. While most artifacts are circa 1800-1930, there is enough variety and educational supplements to make this an impressive display.

While the replica dwellings they built in the museum may be a bit over the top, they still offer a much better view of the people of The Plains than Buffalo Bill ever did.

If Buffalo Bill history and Native American cultures isn't your cup of tea, the museum also houses a fantastic art gallery in the Whitney Western Art Museum. Featuring sculptures and paintings from the American West genre, as well as replicas of the studios used by western art legends Frederic Remmington and Alexander Phimister Proctor, any fan of art will fall in love with this museum. With landscapes, abstracts, wildlife paintings and sculptures, you might just feel inspired to sketch something yourself. Luckily, the museum also has interactive art stations to express yourself.

After appreciating art, make your way to the Draper Natural History Museum for a trip through the vast eco-systems of the region. Over 20,000 square feet of animals and exhibits, you will come away from this museum with a much better understand of the circle of life.

Exhibits include detailed information on geology, wildlife and the human impact on nature. With full sized animals all around, this is a cool place to look at the animals you might not have seen in Yellowstone.

No museum is complete without weapons, and if you need a
dose of awesome weaponry, the Cody Firearms museum will not
disappoint you. Home to the most comprehensive collection of
American firearms in the world, as well as the famed Winchester
Collection, visitors here will be overwhelmed with the number
and variety of guns in America.

No matter your stance on firearms, take a stroll through here to
learn how America became the land of the gun.

Finally, if you get a chance, check out the Harold McCracken Research Library. While you do need an appointment to research in the library, it usually isn't too busy to get in. The library houses over 30,000 books on the region, as well as 400 manuscript collections. If you have ever had a question about the Old West, the answer might be here.

While mainly focusing on Buffalo Bill, the Plains Indians and dude ranching, nearly all the other regional topics, including early exploration of Yellowstone can be found in the collection.

WEST YELLOWSTONE

If you need to get out of the park for a day, but don't want to drive for hours, West Yellowstone is your best chance to find "civilization." The McDonalds (read: free WiFi) and gas stations allow West Yellowstone to also serve as a quick trip to get supplies and check in. Located just 14 miles from Madison Junction in the park, we recommend ducking out this way if you get a chance. Not just for the cheeseburgers and free internet either.

West Yellowstone isn't much to look at, though when you do stand in the main intersection of town, it is easy to see how little the town has changed in the past 100 years. The town was created in 1908 for the sole purpose of welcoming those interested in Yellowstone, and pretty much does the same thing now as it did on day one. Yes, it has been paved and illuminated with lights. Sure, there might be a few hotels and the golden arches visible, but for the most part, the town is still an old west town. With storefronts with swinging doors and raised wooden boardwalks are highlights of the city , the same as it was when trains would arrive daily, escorting visitors into the park

Aside from standard touristy shopping, there are two main attractions in West Yellowstone: the Grizzly & Wolf Discovery Center and the Yellowstone Historic Center. The Grizzly Wolf and Discovery Center is basically an educational zoo, letting you see the size and awesomeness of both wolves and grizzlies. While some may not enjoy the zoo aspect of the Discovery Center, everyone usually walks away with some new knowledge about these two awesome animals. It is also a great stop for those with kids or new to wildlife watching, as the guides and staff do an excellent job helping your trip to the region.

While the Yellowstone Historic Center doesn't sound as exciting as bears and wolves, the history in this museum is a different kind of awesome. The Center focuses on the history of travel to Yellowstone, covering horse and buggies, early cars, airplanes and trains. With six amazing exhibits, spending some time here will help you fully appreciate your road trip even more. If this doesn't sound enticing enough, take a look at a few of the exhibits:

Wings into West

This exhibit features scale models documenting how supplies were flown to this remote, mountain community. This exhibit is full of 80 years of aviation awesomeness. With photos, stories and old advertisements for airlines that flew into the area, this exhibit is pretty good.

Tourist, Trains and the Wonders of Yellowstone

This is a series of pictures documenting the growth of the community of West Yellowstone. Starting in 1872, it documents the region's and cities' role in tourism. The pictures alone make this fantastic.

Stage Coaches and Freight Wagons

Before cars could roll into Yellowstone like it was an everyday thing, the most luxurious way into the park was by stagecoach or wagon. This exhibit has full stagecoaches, including one called the Mount Washburn Special, the only one of this style still in existence.

Wonderland by Train

This exhibit takes a look at the glorious days of train travel. Take a stroll through the old station, look at old train cars and stare dreamily at the old advertisements for Northern Pacific and the other major rail companies.

Dumpster Bears and Old Snaggletooth

Back in the day, Yellowstone used to have daily bear feeding presentations at the dumps around the park. This was so wildly popular that it continued up until the 1960s. While the practice no longer occurs, this exhibit will forever remind us of the silliness our grandparents thought was acceptable. The exhibit also documents the most famous garbage bear of them all, Old Snaggletooth. Seriously, you don't want to miss this.

NOW WHAT?

After an exhaustively long, yet rewarding jaunt around the area, memories have been made, relationships have been strengthened and wilderness has been loved. You have seen one of the best and most unique landscapes in the world. From witnessing erupting geysers to watching wildlife in true wilderness, Yellowstone has been a good trip.

Sure, it might have rained, maybe even snowed, but it snowed on you in Yellowstone. Maybe you hoped to see a wolf, yet did not get the opportunity. The thing about Yellowstone National Park is that it is alive and always changing. It is wild and unpredictable, unscripted and unfolding before your very eyes.

Yellowstone is many things to many people, each connected with something different within the nation's first National Park. For some, it is the wolves, whose newly-restored presence in the park makes it feel a bit more wild and real. For others, it is the smell of geysers in the morning, standing in the Yellowstone River trying their hand at fly-fishing. Each of us has a reason and a story when we first fell in love with Yellowstone.

For me, it was my first bison jam. At 6 years old, being in a small car barely able to see out the window, seeing a bison eye to eye was an exhilarating experience. The herd surrounded our car. My family sat in silence. This was uncharted territory for everyone, but we remained calm. The herd started moving past us, but not before I made eye-contact with a bison that appeared to be as large as our car. I know it sounds lame, but in my head, it was at that moment that I truly experienced a deep connection with nature. Twenty-seven years later, I can still see it vividly in my mind's eye.

Having taken 25 trips to Yellowstone in the 33 years I've been on this planet, it is easy to see that the park is a major part of my life. Sure, not every trip has been perfect, but every single moment in Yellowstone has been memorable. Every trip is different, and every trip turns out to be an indescribable amount of fun.

Now that your road trip is over, it is time to return home with the feeling of a successful trip under your belt. You saw animals, watched geysers erupt and maybe even witnessed a wolf take down a bison or an elk. You may have camped at a remote campground, hiked amazing trails and visited exquisite lodges. You drove the roads, visited the sights and realized that you can't possibly see the entire park in one trip. That is the beauty of Yellowstone.

No matter how many times you return, you will discover a new trail, see a new geyser erupt or witness something you can't even imagine. Keep returning to Yellowstone, encourage your friends and family to travel here and make visiting Yellowstone and all National Parks your new tradition.

I hope you enjoyed this book and it inspired you take take the trip to America's First National Park. If you are reading this from inside Yellowstone National Park, have a great time.

Keep healthy, keep hiking and keep exploring.

Douglas Scott, Exotic Hikes

WELCOME TO YELLOWSTONE

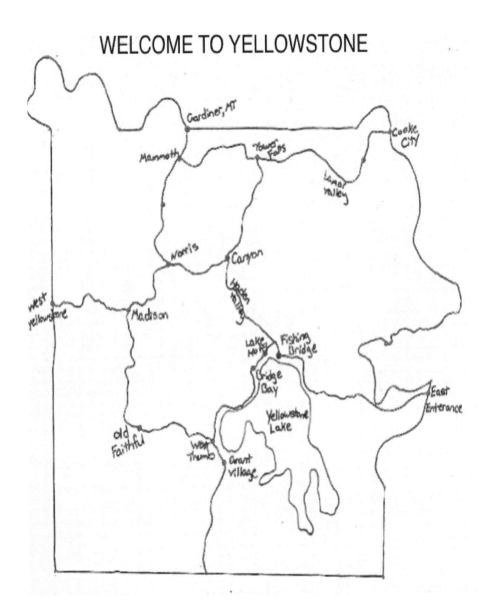

Best Stops

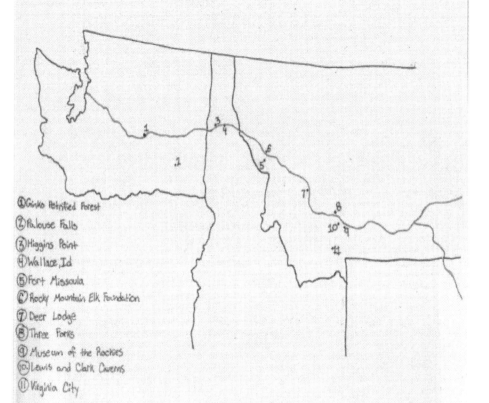

①Ginko Petrified Forest

②Palouse Falls

③Higgins Point

④Wallace, Id

⑤Fort Missoula

⑥Rocky Mountain Elk Foundation

⑦Deer Lodge

⑧Three Forks

⑨Museum of the Rockies

⑩Lewis and Clark Caverns

⑪Virginia City

Quick Stops

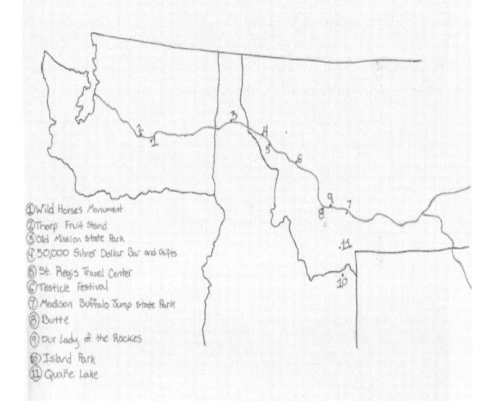

① Wild Horses Monument
② Thorp Fruit Stand
③ Old Mission State Park
④ 50,000 Silver Dollar Bar and Gifts

⑤ St. Regis Travel Center
⑥ Testicle Festival
⑦ Madison Buffalo Jump State Park
⑧ Butte
⑨ Our Lady of the Rockies

⑩ Island Park
⑪ Quake Lake

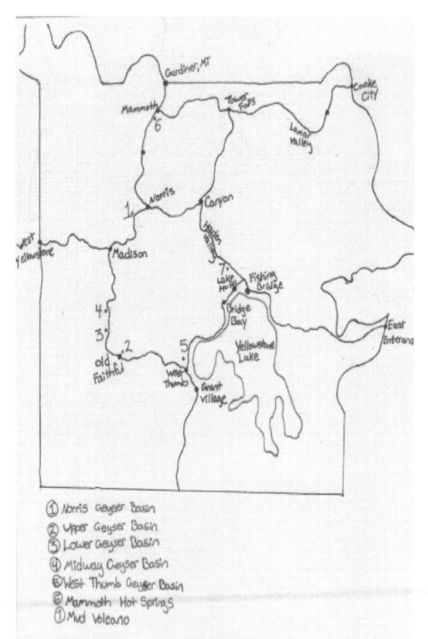

① Norris Geyser Basin
② Upper Geyser Basin
③ Lower Geyser Basin
④ Midway Geyser Basin
⑤ West Thumb Geyser Basin
⑥ Mammoth Hot Springs
⑦ Mud Volcano

Geysers of Yellowstone

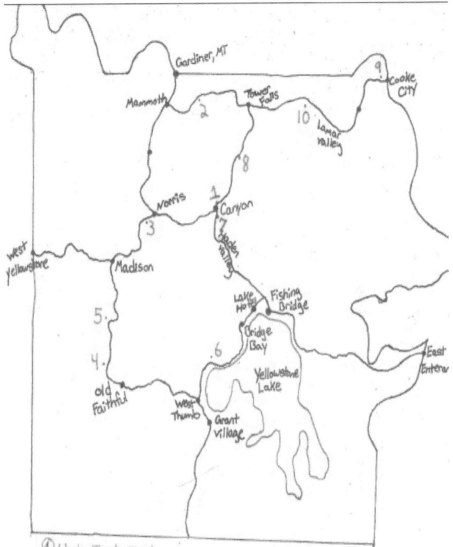

Yellowstone
Hikes

① Uncle Tom's Trail
② Wraith Falls Trail
③ Artist's Paint Pots
④ Mystic Falls
⑤ Fairy Falls
⑥ Elephant Back
⑦ Grand Canyon of Yellowstone
⑧ Mount Washburn
⑨ Pebble Creek
⑩ Speciman Ridge